DIVINE KARMA

The Journey of Self-Discovery

DAVID RAMIREZ

The Journey of Self Discovery

Book One of the Divine Karma Trilogy

ISBN-13: 978-0-9983932-2-3

Divine Karma
13611 South Dixie Hwy. Suite 453
Miami, Florida 33176 USA
www.Divine-Karma.com

DEDICATION

To my cherished family and dear friends, each of whom has touched my life in unique and profound ways, this book is a tribute to you. Your interactions, stories, and unwavering support have inadvertently shaped my perspective, and for that, I am deeply grateful.

To every individual who has crossed my path and shared a piece of their journey with me, know that you've been an integral part of my transformative experience.

But above all, a special dedication to myself, David. It's a rare and courageous act to challenge one's beliefs and embark on a journey of self-discovery. You took that plunge, allowing me to understand the essence of our being and to recognize that every success, every setback, is a narrative we author for ourselves. Your tenacity and introspection have made this book possible, and through these pages, we share the insights gleaned from that personal odyssey.

You've been the quiet warrior in this journey, and today, I take a moment to honor and appreciate your resilience and spirit. Thank you for lighting the way.

Table of Contents

Introduction 5
PART ONE: The Creation 9
Chapter 1 | The Biological Foundation: The Dance of Genetics and Choice 10
Chapter 2 | The Collective Consciousness 22
Chapter 3 | The Interconnected Tapestry of the Human Experience: Minds, Roles, and Shared Narratives 28
Chapter 4 | The Trinity of Truth: Unveiling the Connection 36
PART TWO: The Preservation (Life) 55
Chapter 5 | Unlocking the Chains of Your Mind 58
Chapter 6 | The Spectrum of Awareness 67
Chapter 7 | Belief Is Everything 73
Chapter 8 | The Power of Perception and Creation 86
Chapter 9 | The Ego and Beyond: Sculpting Our Reality and Unraveling Attachments 98
Chapter 10 | The Eternal Equilibrium: Navigating the Dance of Balance and Imbalance 112
PART THREE: The Destruction 120
Chapter 11 | The Real You 121
Chapter 12 | The Tao and the Art of Surrender 136
Chapter 13 | Embracing the Game of Life: The Path to Self-Liberation 150
Chapter 14 | The Man and the Mountain 166
REFERENCES 169
About the Author 171

Introduction

"The Creator created you to one day discover you are the creator." – David Ramirez

When you first entered the world, it was with wide-eyed wonder and amazement. Every sensation, every sound, every color was a marvel waiting to be explored. As an infant, your mind is free from the prejudices, beliefs, and judgments that often cloud adult perception. Think of this stage as the "tabula rasa" phase, a Latin term that means "clean slate." It was a period of purity, unblemished by societal constructs or preconceived notions.

In this phase, you relied heavily on your caregivers, mainly your parents, to guide you and shape your understanding of the world. They played a pivotal role in introducing you to societal norms and values. Like a sponge, your young mind absorbed every lesson, every teaching, and every guideline, many of which aimed to maintain societal equilibrium.

As you grew, you began to understand the dualistic nature of life. There was good and bad, joy and sorrow, light and dark. This realization introduced the concept of choice in your life: how would you react to situations? How would you channel your emotions? These decisions and the consequences they bore often interplayed with the concept of 'karma,' reminiscent of Newton's third law, which states that every action has an equal and opposite reaction.

Imagine if, at our core, we all possess the divine energy of creation. As humans, we embark on a journey, observing and interacting with our creations, feeling intense curiosity and awe. However, as we navigate through life, we begin accumulating beliefs, much like software programs in our subconscious. These beliefs start forming the foundation of our responses and actions.

Fear, an instinct meant to protect us, often becomes a dominant driving force behind many beliefs. It inadvertently builds walls around us, barriers that sometimes hinder our true potential. For example, society might teach us to grieve a certain way, labeling any deviation as inappropriate. But should one celebrate life instead of mourning death, they're seen as defiant.

Our journey through life is dotted with these metaphorical walls. They represent our deep-seated beliefs, some of which might not even serve us anymore. Overcoming these walls doesn't mean finding temporary solutions, like scaling them or digging underneath. It means dismantling them, brick by brick, by challenging and rewriting the scripts that led to their construction.

In essence, nothing is holding you back from realizing your true potential. The barriers, the walls, the limitations: they're all self-imposed. Layers upon layers of beliefs and societal expectations have clouded our vision, making us forget our true essence. But by recognizing and confronting these self-imposed boundaries, you have the power to dissolve them through inner divinity and the law of karma.

The Importance of Inner Divinity and the Law of Karma

Before the majestic theatre of existence opened its curtains, there was us. Enveloped in the serene embrace of darkness, we were a paradox. We were everything and nothing simultaneously, a divine entity awaiting experience. In that stillness, we yearned for an experience, a purpose. Thus, we envisioned the grand spectacle called Life and split our singular essence into what is now eight billion individual consciousnesses. From unity, we descended into diversity. But worry not, for this disconnection is but a temporary phase in our cosmic narrative. Our destiny lies in convergence, in reuniting with our authentic essence. The challenge is simple, yet profound: to remember. Today, dear reader, marks the commencement of our shared voyage toward that remembrance.

In the vast tapestry of human understanding, few concepts are as profoundly woven as that of karma. Its roots burrow into ancient traditions, guiding philosophical thought and spiritual introspection across cultures and epochs.

At the heart of our being lies a spark, an essence, which many term the higher self or inner divinity. It is this intrinsic nature that is capable of elevating our actions and choices. When we synchronize our deeds with this inner divine compass, we steer our life towards higher karmic outcomes. This is not merely a philosophical musing but a profound realization that our alignment with our innermost self can manifest positive karma. It beckons the understanding that divinity is not an external entity but an innate force guiding and resonating within us.

Conversely, just as the physical world operates under undeniable laws, like gravity, the moral universe too pivots around an unerring principle: karma. This cosmic law, transcending time and space, ensures that every action and intention is met with a corresponding consequence. In its vast wisdom and boundless scope, karma functions as the divine fulcrum balancing our moral universe.

Delving into *Divine Karma* is a journey into the heart of these intertwined concepts. It's an exploration that reveals the profound interconnectedness of our choices, their rippling effects, and the cosmic tapestry they weave. As readers, I invite you to understand the profound responsibility our actions carry while also finding solace in the age-old wisdom that the universe, in its divine orchestration, guarantees justice and equilibrium.

In the pages that follow, we shall journey together into the depths of these truths, uncovering the layers of understanding, responsibility, and hope they offer and, ultimately, recognizing the divine dance of karma in our lives. This tome serves as a beacon for those seeking self-realization. You may have stumbled upon these pages in your quest for meaning or, perhaps, mere curiosity. Regardless of the paths that brought you here, I express my gratitude for your presence. Our destinies are intertwined, and this journey is one we are destined to undertake together.

I am no prophet, teacher, or guru. Rather, think of me as a fellow seeker, a comrade joining you on this path, aiding you in navigating the vast expanse of your inner universe. My own pilgrimage towards understanding was instigated by a profound sense of unease, a feeling that much of what I had believed and accepted was, at best, incomplete. I roamed the world, knocking on the doors of wisdom, seeking answers to age-old questions. Yet, it was only when I turned inward that my quest found its resolution. The realization was monumental: the journey wasn't merely about me. It encompassed all of us, every sentient being, and our collective quest for meaning.

To truly fathom our existence, we must investigate our past, origins, and the myriad factors that have culminated in the present moment. Our external world mirrors our internal realm, for we all spring from the same wellspring of consciousness. Our collective endeavor is to know where and how to look and assimilate this newfound knowledge. Uncovering the mysteries of our being and discerning our role in this grand narrative is our shared adventure.

The essence of our story might be deceptively simple or profoundly complex. The epiphanies may strike in a fleeting moment or unfold over a lifetime. Yet, rest assured, understanding will dawn. A future awaits where we live consciously, experiencing life with full awareness, choosing our experiences, and releasing them when they have served their purpose. Although this may sound idealistic, looking the other way perpetuates our world's current chaos.

Our exploration will span various domains, from empirical scientific studies to revered spiritual texts. By juxtaposing diverse perspectives, we aspire to achieve a holistic understanding and discern the interconnectedness at the heart of existence.

However, I implore you to shed any preconceived notions as you tread this path. Let's approach these pages with a fresh, unburdened perspective, setting aside our inherited beliefs. We must distinguish between genuine insights and the inherited dogmas that have shaped our worldview. Question everything. Be it direct observations perceived through our senses or indirect ones gleaned from external sources. Scrutinizing and reflecting will expand our understanding and foster genuine discernment.

This isn't an endeavor to replace your belief system or to amass followers. Instead, it's an invitation. An invitation to dive deep within, to discover the profound wisdom residing in you, to marvel at the intricate tapestry of existence you've woven. This book is merely a tool, a catalyst to awaken your heart and mind, equipping you to live with purpose and in harmony.

As you turn these pages, remember you're embarking on a journey of profound discovery. You will then be armed with newfound wisdom; you will be ready to shape your destiny. The following pages are not a destination but a doorway. What you discover on the other side will depend on what you are willing to question.

PART ONE: The Creation

Chapter 1 | The Biological Foundation: The Dance of Genetics and Choice

Before we explore the vast landscape of consciousness, karma, and collective experience, we must first understand the ground beneath our feet: the self, not as a fixed entity shaped by birth or circumstance, but as a dynamic, responsive system whose very biology answers to belief. Modern science has confirmed what spiritual traditions have long intuited: we are not prisoners of our programming. In this opening chapter, we examine the flexible nature of the human blueprint, and why that flexibility is the door through which every subsequent insight in this book becomes not just possible, but personally available to you.

"Man is what he believes" Anton Chekhov

Chapter 1, inspired by Anton Chekhov's profound assertion, "Man is what he believes," explores the complex relationship between human beings and their biological programming. Building upon the insights from the previous chapter, which compared human and machine intelligence and explored simulated realities, this chapter delves deeper into understanding the essence of human existence. It examines the similarities and differences between humans and computers, focusing on how both are influenced by inherent programming. Importantly, it highlights the unique human ability to transcend these innate limitations, resonating with Dr. Bruce Lipton's transformative work on epigenetics.

The chapter begins with an insightful exploration of our biological foundation, examining the sophisticated code in our DNA. Traditionally seen as a fixed determinant of physical and behavioral traits, the genetic script is now understood as more fluid and adaptable, thanks to epigenetics. Dr. Lipton's work shows that environmental factors and personal beliefs can significantly alter gene expression. This revelation shifts our view of genetics from passive recipients of inherited traits to active participants in their manifestation. It suggests that our experiences and beliefs play a crucial role in shaping our personality, behavior, and even physical health, empowering us with the potential for personal growth and transformation.

Further, the chapter explores the dynamic interplay between our genetic baseline and the multitude of external and internal factors that influence our lives. It presents human development as a process where our genetic code is the starting point, but our experiences and beliefs significantly shape the outcome. This perspective enriches our understanding and opens new personal development and growth avenues.

The chapter then explains the roles played by our environment and experiences in shaping our identity and potential. It highlights the intricate dance between our genetic blueprints and the environmental factors and life experiences we encounter. The formative power of the environment and the dynamic catalysts of life experiences are emphasized, showing how they contribute to our evolving narrative and shape our beliefs, values, and attitudes. This comprehensive view presents human development as a dynamic journey, continuously shaped by the interplay of genetics, environment, and experiences, moving away from a linear, genetically determined path.

"A pivotal focus of the chapter, titled 'Balancing Free Will and Determinism: The Complex Tapestry of Choice and Influence,' explains the intricate concept of free will. It confronts deterministic views, advocating for the human capacity to exercise autonomy in our decision-making processes. Free will is portrayed as the ability to make unique choices that reflect our personal values, aspirations, and beliefs, thus challenging the notion that our biological makeup or past experiences solely predetermine our actions. The chapter explores the theme of conscious decision-making, highlighting the human capability for introspection and self-guided action. In doing so, it emphasizes free will not just as a philosophical concept but as a potent source of empowerment and self-determination. This section of the chapter encourages individuals to assert control over their lives, make decisions aligned with their true selves, and navigate the path toward personal fulfillment and growth. It also acknowledges the counterpoint that 'choice is an illusion,' adding depth to the discussion by considering the extent to which external factors influence our decisions. It invites a nuanced understanding of the balance between free will and determinism."

The chapter then explores the dynamic nature of human potential, significantly informed by advancements in genetics, neuroscience, and psychology. Discoveries in epigenetics and neuroplasticity have reshaped our understanding of the human mind and its potential, suggesting a more fluid and adaptable nature of human capabilities than previously understood. These scientific advancements have profound implications for our perspectives on free will and personal agency, empowering individuals with a renewed sense of control over their destinies.

Finally, the chapter reexamines the concept of biological programming as a catalyst for personal growth and self-awareness. It suggests that understanding our genetic predispositions can enhance our journey of self-discovery and personal development. The chapter emphasizes the importance of recognizing and actively engaging with our genetic predispositions, suggesting that our lifestyle choices can profoundly impact our biological programming. This understanding leads to increased self-compassion and inspires us to take control of our lives, knowing that our actions can modify or even override certain genetic predispositions.

Understanding Our Biological Foundation: The Flexibility of Our Genetic Blueprint

First, we must explore the complexities of our biological makeup, a fundamental aspect of our identity and abilities. This exploration starts with examining the DNA code, which is like a sophisticated script laying the foundation for various physical and behavioral traits. In the past, this genetic script was viewed as a fixed determinant of who we are. However, recent developments in the field of epigenetics have revolutionized this view.

Epigenetics, a field in which Dr. Bruce Lipton has been a pioneer, studies how environmental factors and personal beliefs can alter how our genes are expressed. Unlike the traditional view of genetics, where the DNA sequence is considered unchangeable, epigenetics shows that our genetic potential is more flexible and responsive to our surroundings. This means that various aspects of our lives, from the quality of our relationships and our lifestyle choices to our mental states, can influence our genetic expression. It's a groundbreaking understanding that our genes are not just passive codes but dynamic entities responsive to our life experiences.

This new understanding of genetics offers a more dynamic view, transforming us from passive recipients of our genetic inheritance to active participants in how these traits manifest in our lives. It underlines the importance of life experiences and cultivated beliefs in shaping our personality, behavior, and physical health. The realization that our genetic destiny is not set in stone but rather malleable and changeable is empowering. It suggests that we have more control over our development than previously thought, allowing us to see ourselves as the architects of our lives. This understanding allows us to overcome genetic predispositions and carve out unique paths for ourselves.

The section further explores the intricate relationship between our genetic baseline and the multitude of external and internal factors that influence our lives. It presents human development as a dynamic process. Here, our genetic code is just the starting point, akin to the initial canvas in a painting. The outcome, however, is significantly shaped and colored by our experiences and beliefs. This view enriches our understanding of ourselves and opens new avenues for personal development and growth. It paints a picture of human development as an evolving and interactive process where our inherent genetic potential can be unlocked or altered based on how we live and perceive the world around us.

The Environment and Experience as Sculptors of Identity: Crafting the Self

"The Environment and Experience as Sculptors of Identity: Crafting the Self" in this section provides a deeper insight into how our environment and experiences play crucial roles in shaping our identity and potential. The section explores the subtle yet profound interaction between our genetic blueprints and the environmental factors and life experiences we encounter. This interaction demonstrates that while our genetic predispositions provide a foundational rhythm to our lives, the environment and our experiences ultimately orchestrate the unique performance of our individual lives.

The section emphasizes the significant role of the environment in shaping our genetic expression. It's not just the physical surroundings that impact us but also the social and cultural contexts we find ourselves in. For instance, familial relationships and the broader cultural and social environments leave lasting imprints on our development. For example, a stimulating environment rich in artistic influences can nurture a latent genetic propensity towards creativity, allowing it to flourish.

But the influence of the environment isn't static; it's dynamic and ever-changing. Our life experiences, comprising every interaction, challenge, and achievement we face, act as dynamic catalysts for personal growth. These experiences mold our character and refine our identity, contributing to our evolving narrative. They play a vital role in shaping our beliefs, values, and attitudes. Depending on our experiences, our inherent genetic tendencies can be amplified or redirected, highlighting the fluid and ever-evolving nature of our personal journey.

The section delves into the synergy between nature (our genetics) and nurture (our environment and experiences) in personal development. This exploration reveals that our development is not merely a genetic script written at birth but a complex, responsive process continuously influenced by external and internal factors. This developmental dance is a dynamic dialogue with our genetics, leading to a wide array of developmental outcomes, even among individuals with similar genetic makeups.

Presenting a comprehensive view, the section portrays human development as a dynamic journey continuously shaped by the interplay of genetics, environment, and experiences. This perspective moves beyond the simplistic idea of a linear, genetically predetermined path, revealing a more adaptive and multifaceted process. It highlights the critical importance of our various contexts and experiences, emphasizing their considerable role in defining who we become. This understanding invites a deeper appreciation for the complexity and richness of the human experience, emphasizing the profound impact of our surroundings and choices in sculpting our individual identities. The section underscores that our identities and potentials are not predestined outcomes but are instead formed and continuously reshaped by the myriad influences around us.

Balancing Free Will and Determinism: The Complex Tapestry of Choice and Influence

A central theme of the section focuses on the concept of free will as a fundamental aspect of human psychology. This section challenges deterministic views, which suggest that our biological makeup or past experiences entirely predetermine our actions and life courses. Instead, it posits the idea of free will, emphasizing our ability to exercise autonomy in our decision-making processes.

Free will is portrayed as the capacity to make unique choices that reflect our personal values, aspirations, and beliefs. This perspective acknowledges that while our genetic predispositions and life experiences indeed influence us, these factors do not irrevocably determine our paths. Humans can reflect upon, evaluate, and ultimately choose paths that may diverge from the trajectories suggested by our biology and experiences. This ability is a testament to the human capacity for independent thought and action.

The exploration of free will extends beyond deterministic frameworks, introducing the concept of conscious decision-making. This involves individuals actively assessing their circumstances, contemplating various options, and making choices grounded in rational thought, emotional intelligence, and personal values. This complex cognitive process highlights human introspection and self-guided action, underscoring our ability to think and choose independently.

Recognizing free will goes beyond mere philosophical contemplation; it serves as a powerful tool for empowerment and self-determination. By acknowledging our control over our choices, we instill a sense of personal responsibility and agency. This realization enables individuals to actively engage with their lives, influencing their destinies. This sense of autonomy is integral to our self-concept and drives our pursuit of personal goals and happiness.

Understanding and embracing the concept of free will is also seen as a catalyst for personal growth and development. It encourages individuals to take the reins of their lives, making decisions that align with their true selves and embarking on fulfilling and meaningful paths. This aspect of free will promotes resilience, adaptability, and a proactive approach to navigating life's challenges and opportunities.

Moreover, free will enables individuals to navigate through the complexities and ambiguities of life. It allows for making informed choices in uncertain situations, learning from mistakes, and continually evolving and redefining oneself. This dynamic aspect of human nature underscores our capacity for growth and change, driven by our decisions and actions.

Expanding on the theme of "Free Will: Harnessing the Power of Autonomy and Self-Determination," an intriguing counterpoint often presented in philosophical and psychological discussions is the notion that "choice is an illusion." This perspective challenges the concept of free will, suggesting that the choices we believe we are making freely are, in fact, heavily influenced or even predetermined by a myriad of factors beyond our control.

From this viewpoint, factors such as our genetic predispositions, environmental conditioning, cultural background, and subconscious biases are seen as the true architects of our decisions. For instance, a person's choice in a given situation may feel autonomous, but it could be significantly shaped by their upbringing, societal norms, past experiences, or biological instincts. This perspective argues that these underlying influences operate at a fundamental level that they essentially 'script' our decisions. This leads to the assertion that true free will may not exist as we commonly understand it.

The idea that "choice is an illusion" also intersects with determinism, a philosophical concept that posits every event, including human cognition and behavior, is causally determined by an unbroken chain of prior occurrences. According to this view, our life paths are predetermined by a series of causes and effects, and our perceived choices are merely the outcomes of these pre-existing causes.

Moreover, some neuroscientific studies have suggested that our brains make decisions on a subconscious level before we are even aware of them. These studies often point to the idea that the conscious experience of making a choice is a retrospective construction, a narrative our minds create after the fact.

However, it's crucial to balance this perspective with the understanding of free will discussed in the section. While it's evident that many factors influence our decisions, the concept of autonomy and self-determination is central to human psychology and our sense of self. Many argue that even with external influences, the capacity for self-reflection and conscious decision-making allows for a degree of free will.

The debate between free will and the idea that "choice is an illusion" is ongoing and remains a fundamental question in philosophy, psychology, and neuroscience. It challenges us to consider the extent of our autonomy and confronts us with the complexities of what it means to make a choice. This discussion enriches our understanding of human behavior, encouraging a deeper exploration of the forces that shape our decisions and identities.

The Dynamic Nature of Human Potential: Unveiling the Evolving Self

"The Dynamic Nature of Human Potential: Unveiling the Evolving Self" in this section offers a deep and insightful exploration into the ever-changing landscape of human potential, a journey significantly influenced by groundbreaking advancements in genetics, neuroscience, and psychology. Central to this exploration is Dr. Bruce Lipton's pioneering work in epigenetics, which has fundamentally altered our comprehension of human capabilities, revealing a more fluid and adaptable nature than was previously understood.

The section delves into the concept of epigenetics, which challenges the long-held belief that our genetic code is an immutable determinant of our life's path. Epigenetics reveals that environmental factors, such as our surroundings, lifestyle choices, and even our mental states and beliefs, can profoundly influence gene expression. This means that certain genes can be activated or deactivated based on these factors, indicating that our genetic potential is far more malleable and responsive to external influences than we once thought. This understanding has opened up new perspectives on how our environment and experiences can shape our genetic destiny.

In parallel, the section discusses the concept of neuroplasticity, the brain's remarkable ability to reorganize itself by forming new neural connections throughout life. This adaptability challenges the previously held notion of a static brain, showing that our cognitive and emotional capacities can undergo significant change and development in response to our experiences, learning, and behaviors. Neuroplasticity demonstrates that the brain is not a fixed entity but is dynamic, continuously reshaping itself in response to our interactions with the world.

The synergistic relationship between nature (genetics) and nurture (environment) is beautifully illustrated through these discoveries in epigenetics and neuroplasticity. This interplay suggests that our development and potential are not just the result of our genetic predispositions but are also heavily influenced by our environmental interactions, experiences, and personal choices. These insights provide a holistic view of human development, recognizing the substantial role external factors play in unlocking or redirecting our inherent potential.

These scientific advancements carry significant implications for our understanding of free will and personal agency. They propose that we are not merely passive subjects to our genetic makeup but have the power to influence our own development through our actions, choices, and the environments we create or choose to be in. This empowers individuals with a renewed sense of control over their destinies, highlighting the critical role of personal choice and action in realizing our full potential.

Given these insights, human potential is viewed as a continually evolving entity, constantly being shaped and reshaped by a combination of genetic, environmental, and personal factors. This evolving nature of potential underscores the capacity for growth, adaptation, and transformation inherent in every individual. It challenges the static view of human capabilities and opens up exciting new horizons for personal development and self-actualization.

In summary, the exploration of the dynamic nature of human

potential in this section offers a comprehensive and empowering perspective on human development. It underscores the significant influence of both genetic predispositions and external factors in shaping our abilities and emphasizes the ongoing, adaptable nature of our growth and development. This perspective not only deepens our understanding of ourselves but also motivates us to actively participate in shaping our lives and realizing the immense potential each of us possesses.

Biological Programming as a Catalyst for Growth: Navigating the Terrain of Self-Discovery

"Biological Programming as a Catalyst for Growth: Navigating the Terrain of Self-Discovery" in Chapter 14 presents a nuanced reexamination of the role of biological programming in our lives. It moves beyond the traditional view of genetics as mere determinants of our physical and behavioral traits, proposing instead that our genetic predispositions can serve as powerful catalysts for personal growth and self-awareness. This section posits that a deeper understanding of the inherent programming within our DNA can significantly enhance our journey toward self-discovery and personal development.

The section stresses the importance of recognizing and understanding our genetic predispositions, which act like signposts indicating our inherent strengths and potential areas for improvement. This approach doesn't imply resigning to a predetermined fate; rather, it offers a clearer understanding of our journey's starting points. Understanding why we might be naturally inclined towards certain behaviors, talents, or challenges helps us comprehend how these inclinations influence our interactions with the world and shape our life paths.

Armed with this knowledge, we are better positioned to strategically leverage our innate strengths and be more mindful of areas where we might need additional support or development. For instance, an individual with a genetic predisposition for creativity might seek out environments and opportunities that nurture and stimulate this trait. Conversely, understanding a genetic inclination towards certain health risks could prompt someone to adopt a healthier lifestyle and take preventive measures. This proactive approach to managing our genetic predispositions enhances our well-being and opens avenues for maximizing our potential in different life aspects.

The section advocates for an active engagement with our genetic predispositions, which involves adapting to our inherent traits and, when necessary, challenging them. This could mean someone with a natural tendency toward introversion consciously engaging in social interactions to develop better communication skills. Such active engagement illustrates that, while genetics provide a foundation, our personal choices and efforts significantly influence who we become.

Furthermore, the section delves into the concept of epigenetics and its implications for personal growth. Epigenetics reveals how our environment and behaviors can impact gene expression, suggesting that our lifestyle choices can significantly affect our biological programming. This reinforces the notion that we are not merely passive subjects to our genetic makeup; instead, we have the agency to influence how our genes express themselves through our actions and choices.

In the realm of personal development, the insights gained from understanding our biological programming can be transformative. They lead to increased self-compassion as we recognize that certain aspects of our personality or tendencies are deeply ingrained in our biology. Simultaneously, this understanding inspires us to take control of our lives, knowing that our actions can modify or even override some genetic predispositions.

The section presents a comprehensive and insightful exploration of various facets of human development and potential, weaving together the themes of genetic influences, environmental factors, free will, and personal growth.

At its core, the section challenges the traditional view of biological programming as a mere determinant of physical and behavioral traits. It introduces the concept of epigenetics, highlighting how environmental factors and personal beliefs can significantly influence gene expression. This revelation shifts our understanding of genetics from a rigid script to a dynamic and adaptable code, emphasizing that our genetic potential is more malleable and responsive to external influences than previously thought.

The section also delves into the brain's neuroplasticity, illustrating its remarkable ability to reorganize and form new neural connections throughout life. This adaptability contradicts the notion of a static brain and demonstrates our capacity for significant cognitive and emotional development in response to experiences, learning, and behavior.

Central to the section is the exploration of free will. It challenges deterministic views that suggest our actions are wholly predetermined by our biology and past experiences, advocating instead for our ability to exercise autonomy in decision-making. Free will is portrayed as the capacity to make choices that reflect our personal values, aspirations, and beliefs. The section balances this with the perspective that choice can be influenced or even predetermined by factors beyond our control, like genetic predispositions and environmental conditioning, adding depth to the discussion on the balance between free will and determinism.

The final section of the section emphasizes the role of biological programming as a catalyst for personal growth and self-awareness. It encourages readers to recognize and engage with their genetic predispositions, not as limitations but as starting points for growth and self-exploration. This understanding, combined with the insights from epigenetics, empowers individuals to take control of their lives and shape their destinies.

In summary, the section offers a nuanced and multifaceted view of human development. It provides a compelling argument for the dynamic interplay between genetics, environment, and personal choice in shaping our identities and potentials. The section concludes with a message of empowerment, urging readers to embrace their unique genetic makeup and the vast potential for growth and self-discovery that lies within each individual.

Chapter 2 | The Collective Consciousness

With the individual self established as a malleable, belief-responsive system, we can now turn to the larger field in which that self participates. No individual is an island. The collective consciousness (the vast, shared reservoir of human experience, intuition, and knowledge) shapes every thought we believe is entirely our own.

"We are like islands in the sea, separate on the surface but connected in the deep." – William James

At the core of our interwoven tales and experiences lies the intriguing concept of the collective consciousness. This profound bond acts as a thread, intricately stitching together our memories of the past, the feelings of the present, and our hopes for the future. Envision it as an immense, cosmic library, a reservoir overflowing with the knowledge and understanding of every conceivable subject, and it's accessible to all. When we engage with the collective consciousness, we're essentially plugging into a vast network of shared experiences, profound insights, and invaluable lessons accumulated over millennia. These form the foundation for our daily decisions, behaviors, and emotional responses.

Consider the simple reflex of recoiling from a heated object or the innate sense of danger from consuming something toxic. These instincts aren't just individual learning but are shaped by centuries of shared human experience archived in the collective consciousness. This reservoir not only influences our actions but helps forge our intuitive sense, guiding us even when we're unaware.

However, recognizing the collective consciousness's evolutionary nature is essential. It isn't a fixed or static compendium of knowledge. Instead, it grows, changes, and transforms with us. Early human civilizations' beliefs, knowledge, and worldviews differed from those during the Renaissance. Similarly, the insights of the contemporary digital era vastly differ from those of previous generations. As we grow, learn, and evolve, the collective consciousness captures these shifts, thus becoming a dynamic reflection of humanity's journey through time.

Interconnected Minds: Exploring the Hive Mind in Collective Consciousness and Human Evolution

The concept of a collective consciousness, often described with the metaphor of a "hive mind," is not merely an inactive collection of shared human experiences. Instead, it's a dynamic, thriving network that shapes the way we think, act, and evolve as a species. This network doesn't just record our collective past; it actively changes, influencing people across time and space.

"Hive mind" comes from observing bees, which seem to work together as if they have a single mind. For humans, it means that our collective thoughts, feelings, and actions can converge, leading to common knowledge and behaviors within a group. It's a way to explain how human understanding isn't fixed but is constantly evolving, actively shaping our society.

The "100th monkey phenomenon," noted in Japan in 1952, demonstrates this idea. It showed that a new behavior, like a monkey washing potatoes, spread beyond the immediate group to others far away who couldn't have learned it directly. This isn't just about animal behavior; it highlights how our collective consciousness can extend across distances and even different species.

This phenomenon implies that when enough individuals adopt a behavior, it becomes part of the species' collective knowledge, no matter the physical distance between them. It points to a process where information is shared in a way that goes beyond individual learning.

By suggesting that there is a point where shared information integrates almost instantly into collective understanding, this concept ties back to the hive mind. It proposes that the development of societies and even other species might rely on this shared consciousness. It presents the fascinating possibility that all life is connected through a network of consciousness that shapes how we live and interact.

The Global Consciousness Project, which employed random number generators around the world, sought to measure this phenomenon. Remarkably, these devices showed unusual patterns during significant global events, like the tragic events of September 11, 2001. This suggests that collective human emotions could resonate worldwide, potentially affecting even our technology.

Finally, common fears across different cultures, such as the fear of heights or spiders, may not be individual concerns but rather ingrained parts of our collective psyche. These widespread fears, present even in people with no related traumatic experiences, might be inherited from our ancestors, embedded warnings that have become part of our collective consciousness through centuries of human evolution.

Modern Systems and the Natural World: Shaping the Hive Mind and Consciousness

In this technological era, it's vital to understand that the "hive mind," a term once associated only with organic origins, is now significantly shaped by modern systems like media. These platforms can do more than disseminate information; they hold the profound ability to intensify, skew, or outright manipulate collective fears, beliefs, and perceptions. Take arachnophobia, a fear with evolutionary roots: media can exacerbate this fear, using sensationalist portrayals that may deepen collective anxieties. This underscores the need to engage with the concept of collective consciousness not just academically but practically, utilizing it to navigate our complex, media-saturated world more consciously. By doing so, we can strive for a collective psyche that is informed, balanced, and decidedly forward-thinking.

Nature's Role in Collective Balance

Paralleling the artificial is nature's grand blueprint, an intricate web of designs and systems that crucially shapes our collective consciousness. It's a blueprint characterized by constant evolution, a perpetual dance of adaptation to new challenges. For example, when nature encounters a barren patch of earth, it doesn't passively accept this disruption. It may initiate regrowth or introduce new species to regain balance. This restorative impulse is not just evident in the plant kingdom but is echoed in animal behaviors and ecosystem dynamics. Humans, too, are an integral thread in nature's tapestry. Our fundamental drives, like survival and reproduction, interplay with nature's equilibrium, often in ways we only partially understand. Even the hardships we face, such as diseases or natural disasters, can be seen as part of nature's way of maintaining balance, ensuring our species doesn't compromise the health of the broader ecosystem.

The rebound of wildlife around the Chernobyl site after the catastrophic nuclear disaster is a testament to this resilient balancing act. The return of flora and fauna to an area once deemed lost to radioactive desolation speaks volumes of nature's capacity for recovery and balance, a stark and hopeful contrast to the potential disarray sown by technological influence.

The Dualistic Nature of Consciousness: Insights from Alan Watts

Alan Watts, a visionary philosopher, introduced an enlightening perspective on consciousness by delineating it into two types: spotlight and floodlight consciousness. The "spotlight" consciousness is akin to a focused beam of light on a stage, illuminating a single actor, a metaphor for the intense, singular attention we're encouraged to develop from childhood. Our education systems and societal norms emphasize this spotlight, directing us to concentrate on one task or thought, ignoring all else.

Contrastingly, the "floodlight" consciousness is the diffused glow that softly illuminates the entire stage, allowing for a more holistic view. It resembles our ability to maintain an expansive, all-encompassing awareness, managing to drive a car while immersed in deep conversation, for instance. This form of consciousness operates in the periphery, subtly orchestrating a multitude of tasks and perceptions, yet it's often undervalued in a society that prizes the sharp focus of the spotlight.

Both forms of consciousness are integral to our experience of life. The spotlight allows us to navigate specific challenges and tasks, while the floodlight provides a rich, nuanced backdrop of understanding and perception. As we grapple with the forces of media and nature that shape our collective hive mind, acknowledging and valuing both types of consciousness can lead to a more harmonious, aware existence, one that honors the richness of both the individual and the collective experience.

The Mystical Experience: Awakening the Floodlight

A profound realization awaits those who tap into their floodlight consciousness. This realization often manifests as a mystical or cosmic experience, an awakening to the interconnectedness of all things. Those who attain this state, which Buddhists term "bodhi" and Hindus call "moksha," recognize their true, universal self. This self isn't a separate entity but the entirety of existence, the cosmos itself.

This vast universe, which is essentially us in our most profound form, has the ability to express itself in countless ways: each person, each creature, every star and planet is an expression of this universal dance. Each existence is a unique game the universe plays, from the human experience to the fluttering of a butterfly.

The true tragedy, Watts suggests, is our collective forgetfulness. Raised in a culture that prioritizes the spotlight, we lose sight of our floodlight, our broader connection to the universe. Yet, it's crucial to remember that each of us is an integral part of this vast cosmic dance. Every individual and creature represents the universe experiencing itself in myriad forms. By recognizing and valuing both our spotlight and floodlight consciousness, we can begin to truly understand our place in the cosmos.

The Mechanics of Spotlight Consciousness: How We Focus and Ignore

In the intricate ballet of our consciousness, the spotlight is a guiding force, directing our attention with precision. But how exactly does this mechanism of focus work?

Our brain is constantly bombarded with stimuli. From the ambient hum of a fan to the soft rustling of leaves outside, from the touch of fabric against our skin to the myriad thoughts that dance through our mind, all these vie for our attention. However, our brain needs to prioritize to function efficiently, especially in complex environments.

Think of the brain's attention as a vigilant gatekeeper. Amidst the clamor of stimuli, this gatekeeper uses the spotlight of our consciousness to selectively focus on what is deemed most pertinent at a given moment. This selective attention is biologically advantageous. By focusing on a specific stimulus, we can respond more effectively to immediate demands, whether catching a ball, listening intently to someone, or reading a line of text.

However, this sharp focus comes with a trade-off. To accentuate the object of our attention, the background, or less immediate stimuli, must be relegated, toned down, or, in some cases, completely ignored. Doing so doesn't mean the brain isn't processing the background; rather, it's assigning it a lower priority. Thus, while you're engrossed in a gripping novel, you might not notice the ticking of a clock, even though you still register it subconsciously.

This intense, directed form of attention, or spotlight consciousness, as elucidated by Alan Watts, isn't just a cerebral mechanism; it's deeply interwoven with our cultural fabric. We're conditioned to champion this concentrated focus, often at the expense of the broader, more encompassing floodlight consciousness. While the spotlight helps us navigate intricate tasks and complex interactions, the floodlight connects us to the expansive tapestry of existence, reminding us of our place within the grand cosmic dance. Recognizing the value and function of both types of consciousness is crucial for a more complete understanding of ourselves and our relationship with the universe.

Chapter 3 | The Interconnected Tapestry of the Human Experience: Minds, Roles, and Shared Narratives

"Alone we can do so little; together we can do so much." – Helen Keller

Every individual's journey mirrors the vast experiences that define the human condition. While each person's perspective is unique, we're all actors in the grand theatre of life, playing distinct roles. Each part we play and every decision we make ultimately shape the larger narrative, impacting everyone around us. The ancient proverb, "What we sow in others, we reap in ourselves," holds profound truth. Our perceptions of separateness often obscure our interconnectedness. Yet, if we trace back our existence, it becomes evident that we all originated from a singular source. Whether viewed from a spiritual perspective or even a dogmatic religious one, the underlying truth remains: we are interconnected, and the spaces between us bridge rather than divide.

Understanding this profound connection requires delving into what makes each human experience unique: our mind.

The Mind: An Orchestra of Thoughts and Senses

Our minds are powerful generators of reality, crafting our perceptions through thoughts. Every heartbeat, every breath, and every sensory experience is a manifestation of thought. Our senses are the tools we deploy to decipher the world around us. They inform our thoughts and, in turn, our reality. Hence, understanding how our minds function is paramount to understanding our unique experiences.

Our perceptions sculpt the universe we inhabit. If we perceive our surroundings as threatening, our reality mirrors that perception. Conversely, seeing every situation as a lesson transforms even adversities into opportunities for growth. We often label experiences as good or bad, but these labels are mere constructs of the mind.

Embracing the idea that each experience offers a lesson allows us to find value in every situation.

This perspective, while conceptually straightforward, is challenging to implement. Understanding that our thoughts mold our reality is one thing; identifying and reshaping those thoughts is another. This journey of self-awareness, both individual and collective, necessitates a deep dive into the mind.

The "Oceanic Feeling"

Romain Rolland's term, "oceanic feeling," beautifully captures the sensation of boundless connection reminiscent of an expansive ocean. This concept gained traction when Sigmund Freud, the father of psychoanalysis, explored its implications. This feeling epitomizes an infant's deep connection to its mother, a period when the self hasn't differentiated from others. Though this pure sense of unity diminishes as we mature, vestiges of it linger. Freud postulated that humans inherently seek this sense of unity, often manifesting in group affiliations, especially religious ones.

Freud's study of the human psyche delved deeper than just our collective inclinations; he also sought to unravel the intricacies of individuality. He postulated that our behaviors stem from interactions between three components: the id, the ego, and the superego.

The id, driven by primal instincts, craves immediate satisfaction. The ego, rooted in reality, mediates between the id's desires and societal norms, ensuring our behaviors align with accepted standards. Meanwhile, the superego is our moral compass, guided by societal expectations and lessons from authority figures.

These components, shaped by our environments and cultures, craft our behaviors and experiences. The ego, our reality mediator, also limits us, setting boundaries based on societal expectations. Recognizing these limitations is crucial for growth, as they often stem from ingrained beliefs. Pushing these boundaries, questioning societal norms, and redefining our beliefs can lead to personal and collective evolution.

Examining the interplay of the identity, ego, and superego in our lives can be enlightening. Reflect on your inherent desires and the societal filters they pass through before action. Are these filters based on personal experiences or inherited beliefs? By confronting and understanding these constructs, we can redefine our reality.

To test our perceptions further, consider a simple taste test. With your senses inhibited, how well can you truly identify flavors? This exercise underscores how our minds prioritize existing knowledge over immediate experience. Such ingrained patterns shape our perceptions, often skewing them towards the familiar.

In conclusion, the human experience is a tapestry of individual threads woven into the vast fabric of the collective. Understanding the mind's workings, challenging our perceptions, and recognizing our interconnectedness can enrich our personal journeys while contributing positively to the collective narrative.

The Nature of Problems: It's All About Perspective

When we talk about facing a problem, it's essential to understand that problems are not inherently present in situations or events. Instead, they arise from our perception of those situations. In other words, the primary issue is often not the situation itself but how we view and interpret it.

Our minds are conditioned to identify and label challenges from a young age. When we encounter a situation that doesn't align with our expectations or beliefs, we categorize it as a problem. And once labeled, our instinctual response is to resist or oppose it. This opposition is what gives energy and validation to the issue, solidifying its status as a problem in our minds.

Perceiving a challenge is only the beginning. Our immediate and conditioned reaction to it can often exacerbate the situation. By instinctively responding or reacting to a perceived problem, we end up feeding it, giving it more power and significance than it might inherently possess. This reaction can drain our energy, and more often than not, this approach fails to offer a genuine solution.

Shifting Your Perspective

However, there's another way to navigate these challenges. Instead of automatically reacting to a problem, consider reshaping your viewpoint. Ask yourself: Is this situation genuinely problematic, or does my perception make it so? Instead of avoiding or resisting the issue, confront it head-on. Break it down, examine its components, and recognize it for what it truly is: a situation that challenges your pre-existing beliefs or expectations.

By being mindful and aware of your experience, you allow yourself the opportunity to learn from it. It shifts the focus from the problem to the lesson it brings, enabling you to regain the power you've unconsciously surrendered.

Each challenge or problem we face comes with its own set of lessons. Understanding and appreciating these lessons can release any attachment to the perceived problem. This act of letting go not only frees you from the constraints of the issue but also empowers you.

In every challenge or problem, there's an inherent solution. It often involves changing our perspective, understanding the lessons the situation brings, and adjusting our reactions. Remember, it's not the situation that's problematic but how we choose to perceive and respond to it.

Within the heart of every challenge lies the seed of resolution, a hidden kernel of opportunity that awaits only the shift of our gaze. Our perspective is the lens through which we view the trials we face; to adjust the focus is to transform the obstacle into a stepping stone. Each problem, therefore, is not just a blockade but a classroom, rich with lessons poised to guide us toward growth and deeper understanding.

This dance of perception and reality is the crux of karma, the cosmic principle that our actions and intentions are not fleeting but cyclical forces that return to us, often transformed and instructive. It is in our response to life's hurdles that karma finds its canvas, painting the future with the strokes of our present deeds and attitudes.

When we encounter a problem, if we choose to meet it with resistance and negativity, we may unknowingly invite similar energy back into our lives, perpetuating a cycle that reinforces the very barriers we seek to overcome. However, by approaching our challenges with a spirit of openness, eager to learn from the difficulty and ready to adapt our reactions, we engage positively with the karmic cycle. We send forth ripples of positivity and growth that are likely to return to us in kind.

Thus, our perception, the lessons we glean, and our reactions are intimately connected, weaving together the tapestry of our experience. By consciously choosing our perspective, embracing life's lessons, and reacting with intention, we not only navigate our current challenges more effectively but also shape the karmic path that lies ahead, paving the way for a future rich with wisdom and well-being.

Understanding Karma and Achieving Balance

Buddhism emphasizes the principle of karma, a concept rooted deeply in understanding desire and attachment. The Second Noble Truth identifies desire as the primary cause of suffering. At its core, desire leads to attachment. Buddha, recognizing this, preached liberation from desire and attachment, advocating for adopting the Middle Way.

The Middle Way or Middle Path is more than just a lifestyle. It's a state of being devoid of attachments, transcending biases and judgments. In this balanced state, one resides in one's authentic and natural self, free from the influences of external circumstances and internal emotions.

Venturing outside this natural state, succumbing to desires, or forming attachments sets the stage for karma. Originating from the Sanskrit word "karma," which translates to "action," karma represents the universal principle of cause and effect. It dictates that every action elicits a reaction. This balance is often visualized as a scale. When you act on a desire or form an emotional attachment, you tip the scale, creating an imbalance. It's not the object of desire but the act of seeking it that disrupts this equilibrium. Thus, every action and every choice influenced by the ego disturbs our inherent balance.

To restore this balance, one must release both the desire and the emotional attachment. Doing so liberates the associated karma, preventing the accrual of "karmic debt." This debt, if accumulated, ensures recurring experiences until the debt is "settled" or the karma is balanced out. Such experiences often manifest as life lessons, pushing us to confront our actions, understand their implications, and grow from them.

Our lives are rich tapestries of experiences. While seemingly enriching, emotional attachments to these experiences can lead to karmic imbalances. Recognizing and understanding this dynamic is pivotal for living in harmony with oneself and the world.

A prevalent misconception is that emotional attachments enhance our experiences, making them more meaningful. Love, for instance, is a profound emotional attachment. But when love becomes the source of pain, it leads to suffering, a direct consequence of karmic debt.

Ultimately, all karmic debts demand settlement. Some may be challenging and painful, but over time, with understanding and detachment, one gains wisdom. Achieving harmony and breaking free from the karmic cycle signifies liberation. In Sanskrit, this state of ultimate freedom is termed 'Nirvana' or 'Moksha.'

Nature epitomizes balance. Unlike humans, animals and plants exist without the confines of constructed beliefs or existential anxieties. Often rooted in human-made constructs, these anxieties create a perceived dichotomy between us and nature. In truth, we are intrinsic parts of nature, interconnected and interdependent. Our innate state mirrors nature's balance. Disturbances arise only when we deviate, allowing emotions to cloud our experiences.

While ambition and purpose drive human existence, aligning these with our true nature is vital. When they diverge, karmic experiences emerge. Adopting a fluid approach to life, akin to water in a river, guides us seamlessly through our journey. Resistance, be it against life's flow or inherent nature, only amplifies suffering.

Embracing this understanding lets one observe life's myriad experiences harmoniously. When emotions arise, awareness ensures their transient nature is recognized, allowing for detachment. Like appreciating a flower's fragrance without feeling the need to pluck it or experiencing a play's emotions without lingering attachment, life too can be lived fully yet freely.

In our shared existence, individual karmas intertwine, shaping our collective reality. Recognizing our profound interconnectedness, even oneness, completes our existential circle, aligning us with the collective consciousness and elevating our awareness.

Exploring the Power of Questioning: A Guide to Truth and Reality

Questioning, an art as ancient as human cognition, is the foundation of our quest for understanding. As we delve into this exploration, it's crucial to familiarize ourselves with some influential methods of inquiry that have shaped philosophical thought over millennia. These methodologies offer a framework for questioning and valuable insights into the very nature of truth and reality.

Socrates, the revered Athenian philosopher, believed that truth was an invaluable treasure that could only be unearthed through reason and logic. His method of dialogical argumentation involved presenting a thesis, challenging it with an antithesis, and ultimately arriving at a synthesis. This iterative discovery process is reminiscent of the Hegelian dialectic formulated by Georg Wilhelm Friedrich Hegel. The dialectic posits that a thesis, upon encountering its antithesis, evolves into a synthesis, becoming a new thesis in a ceaseless spiral of refinement. The ultimate goal? To uncover an unequivocal truth, the absolute synthesis.

A noteworthy mention is Nagarjuna, a second-century Buddhist philosopher, who ingeniously employed the dialectic to conclude that existence itself is multi-faceted: "All things exist; all things do not exist; all things both exist and do not exist; all things neither exist nor do not exist." Such profound introspection demonstrates that the essence of questioning transcends the binary boundaries of logic, inviting a deeper exploration of human thought.

René Descartes, the vanguard of modern philosophy, aptly stated, "I think, therefore I am." Yet, his more profound insight suggests, "If you would be a real seeker after truth, it is necessary that at least once in your life you doubt, as far as possible, all things." Descartes propounded that to discern the truth, one must be willing to scrutinize everything, accepting only the irrefutable.

Siddhartha Gautama, known to the world as Buddha, echoed this sentiment. He encouraged discernment based on firsthand knowledge rather than hearsay, traditions, or assumptions: "When you know for yourselves... then you should enter and remain in them."

Consider the timeless question: Does God exist? Drawing from Nagarjuna, we find multifaceted answers. Socrates might deflect with a counter-question, while Descartes would delve into existential introspection. Buddha's approach would be to reflect inward, seeking personal understanding. The overarching realization? Our perception of God, or any concept for that matter, hinges on individual beliefs and the methodologies employed to explore them. Perhaps the existence of God is not an external truth but rather a personal revelation shaped by one's own beliefs and experiences.

While the methods presented are invaluable, they merely serve as guides. Embracing these techniques will empower you to critically evaluate your beliefs, paving the way for profound self-realization. This journey of introspection and discovery is fundamental for growth and enlightenment, especially as you navigate the pages of this book.

"In the grand mosaic of cosmic understanding, it is only the unenlightened who perceive Vishnu, Shiva, and Brahma as distinct entities. In reality, they represent the universe's eternal cycle: creation, preservation, and destruction. This trinity, the Trimurti, embodies the essence of existence, resonating within every being. Those truly awakened perceive no divisions, recognizing the universal spirit in all. True wisdom lies in transcending these apparent divisions and acknowledging the omnipresent unity."

~ A deeper exploration of Vishnu's discourse on the Nature of the Trinity (Trimurti) ~

Chapter 4 | The Trinity of Truth: Unveiling the Connection

"Truth is not something outside to be discovered, it is something inside to be realized." – Osho

The Trinity of Truth is not a mere concept but a profound realization of the human psyche. It draws a triad, bridging religion, science, and spirituality. One finds the intrinsic truth at its center: a profound understanding of humanity and its existence on Earth. This triad, when acknowledged, can be the pathway to aligning oneself with the broader consciousness or a trap that keeps one tethered to the mundane.

Inherently, every individual perceives their reality through the lenses of one or more of these disciplines. These branches shape our core beliefs. A common misconception is to view these disciplines as standalone entities, often at odds with each other. Yet, despite their distinct methodologies and teachings, they converge towards a central truth.

Historically, we've been ensnared in the illusion of separation, pitting ideologies against one another and allowing such divisions to manifest as conflicts: against each other, nature, and within ourselves. This perceived divide is a mere illusion of our making. Just as the space between two objects both separates and connects them, our perceived differences are bridges to our deeper shared truths.

One undeniable truth that emerges from these realms is the unity of creation: every being stems from a singular source. This source has been named differently across cultures: the Universe, Creator, Source, and, commonly, God. The nature or form of this source is immaterial. The crux is the realization of a universal force or energy responsible for all existence. Accepting this truth forms the cornerstone of understanding the interplay of the trinity.

As you journey through these revelations, it's essential to maintain a healthy skepticism, questioning and analyzing the ideas presented. However, recognizing the singular source of all creation is paramount. This understanding can potentially transform individual consciousness, leading to a harmonized collective awareness.

Throughout history, in religious texts, scientific discoveries, and spiritual teachings, there are hints (breadcrumbs, if you will) that guide us toward understanding our interconnectedness. To genuinely decipher these clues, one must strip away preconceived notions and view the world with an open heart and mind. Blind acceptance of any belief limits one's ability to discern more profound truths.

It's worth noting that many beliefs and dogmas have historically been propagated to control the masses. Leaders can easily wield influence by instilling fear and endorsing views that bolster such fears. Such tactics, meant initially to navigate treacherous times, evolved into tools of power, alienating those who dared to think differently.

Blind adherence is a path paved in fear. To live fearlessly is to realize that most fears are constructs of our minds, often rooted in past experiences or apprehensions of the future. Such fears confine us, restricting our potential. By recognizing these self-imposed chains, one can begin to break free from the cycle of fear and suffering.

Suffering, in essence, is our attachment to desires. But our true nature is balance. Embracing our experiences without being emotionally tethered allows us to interact with life more authentically. Recognizing our patterns of attachment and desire is the first step towards releasing them. When we hold onto emotional pain, it often manifests physically in our bodies. We can free ourselves from their weight by understanding and releasing these emotional burdens.

In conclusion, the Trinity of Truth is an invitation to dive deep into understanding the interconnectedness of life's various facets. By embracing this interconnectedness and recognizing the unity of all existence, we can step into a more enlightened, harmonious, and aware existence.

Navigating the profound realization of the human psyche that the Trinity of Truth presents, we understand that it does not encourage a mere academic exercise. Rather, it invites us into a deep communion with the essence of existence, which has been, for centuries, explored through various channels. One such profound channel is religion.

Religion: A Deeper Understanding

Transitioning from the overarching view of the Trinity, we come to contemplate one of its integral components: Religion. At its core, religion represents "a system of beliefs that individuals adhere to with fervor and faith." This domain is not isolated; it intertwines intricately with science and spirituality, seeking answers to the same fundamental questions about the origins, nature, and purpose of existence. Many believe these answers are revealed through a divine entity or entities, and it is through this lens that we attempt to discern the shape and structure of the source at the heart of the Trinity of Truth.

Religion, in its myriad forms, strives to offer guidance on how to navigate the human experience. It establishes rituals, devotions, and moral frameworks aimed at steering human actions and behaviors. It's within these organized structures (whether they are led by a Pope, as in Catholicism, or take on different hierarchies) that communities find common ground, shared values, and a sense of belonging.

As we delve into the specifics of religious beliefs and practices, it is essential to carry with us the understanding of the interconnectedness that the Trinity of Truth elucidates. It reminds us that while organized religions offer a path to divine understanding, they are but one aspect of the complex tapestry of our existence, inherently linked to the broader consciousness that encompasses all.

At its core, religion represents "a system of beliefs that individuals adhere to with fervor and faith." This domain delves into understanding the origins, nature, and purpose of existence, which many believe stems from a divine entity or entities. Religion aims to guide human actions and behaviors through rituals, devotions, and moral frameworks.

In many instances, religion takes the form of an organized structure. Organized religions have established tenets and rituals that bind communities together. Such structures are led by defined hierarchies, like the Rabbi in Judaism. "Organized religion" often refers to globally recognized religious factions with which one can officially affiliate.

My perspective on religion largely encompasses organized religions rooted in Abrahamic, East Asian, and Indian traditions. I perceive religion as a roadmap for individuals to navigate their lives, considering the potential rewards or consequences in the afterlife. This journey often involves comparing our actions with those depicted in sacred texts like the Bible or the Quran. Such texts significantly influence our moral compass. Yet, it's crucial to recognize that total and unquestioning faith in these narratives can lead to blind obedience, often in pursuit of divine approval and the afterlife's promised rewards.

Despite this, religious teachings offer profound insights into human nature. Let's delve into some specific verses and their interpretations.

The Divinity Within Us

The Bible has been a guiding force for humanity over centuries. Despite its widespread influence, its teachings are often misinterpreted. One of its core messages is the assertion that humans were crafted in God's likeness. This implies our inherent divine nature and our creative capabilities. To some, this statement might sound blasphemous. However, verses such as Luke 17:21 in the King James Version state, "The kingdom of God is within you." Although different translations exist, the core message remains consistent: divinity is omnipresent, both externally and internally. Our essence is, thus, a reflection of the creator, making each individual inherently divine.

History has shown that societies have feared questioning the idea of a higher power demanding absolute allegiance. Such doctrines often emphasized an external divine entity, pushing the idea that humans were merely subservient entities. However, the true power and divinity lie within each of us.

The Story of Adam, Eve, and Duality

Genesis offers insights into the human psyche's creation, representing the ego's birth and our separation from our divine core. While Adam was initially singular, Eve's creation introduced duality, representing contrasting aspects of human nature. This duality is further emphasized by their actions surrounding the Tree of Knowledge. Their consumption of the fruit symbolizes humanity's detachment from its divine essence.

Art and philosophy often touch upon this theme. Michelangelo's iconic "The Creation of Adam" in the Sistine Chapel could be interpreted to represent the duality within us. Observations like the background resembling the human brain suggest deeper symbolism about humanity's inherent divine nature and interconnectedness.

Power of Creation: Light and Darkness

Embracing our divine nature means acknowledging our creative power. As God is believed to have forged both light and darkness, as humans, we, too, possess the ability to create both good and evil. This duality is integral to the human experience. Religious doctrines reflect this by representing both divine and malevolent forces. However, it's crucial to recognize that both exist within us.

The key lies in understanding this inherent duality without passing judgment. Recognizing and accepting both sides of our nature allows us to lead balanced lives. Our thoughts and beliefs shape our realities, so it's essential to approach life holistically, acknowledging all facets of our existence.

In summary, religion offers a framework for understanding our place in the world and our inherent divinity. By delving deeper into religious texts and interpretations, we can better understand ourselves and our potential.

Religion, with its rich narratives and doctrines, invites us to consider the broader questions of our existence and to embrace our place within a divinely orchestrated universe. It beckons us to explore deeper meanings and to interpret the teachings that have been handed down through the ages. In doing so, it reveals layers of understanding about our inner selves and our expansive potential. However, the journey to comprehension does not halt at the boundaries of the spiritual or the mystical.

Science: Understanding through Questioning

As we pivot from the introspective truths that religion imparts, we enter the realm of science, where our quest for understanding continues in a different light. Science stands as the beacon of methodical inquiry, stripping down the universe to its fundamental components. It's a realm that values the systematic acquisition of knowledge, utilizing observation and experimentation as its chisels to sculpt our understanding of the material world.

Much like the religious pursuit of divinity, science seeks to unravel the tapestry of the cosmos, albeit through empirical evidence and repeatable proofs. Newtonian Physics, a cornerstone of modern science, has provided a framework much like religious texts do, enabling us to decrypt the mechanical nature of the universe at the most granular level, from cells to atoms.

Both religion and science, in their own profound yet distinctive ways, guide us toward a more comprehensive grasp of the universe and our place within it. As we transition from the contemplative reflections of religion to the empirical investigations of science, we carry forward a sense of awe and a hunger for truth, eager to piece together the grand puzzle of existence using every tool at our disposal.

At its core, science is the systematic acquisition of knowledge about the physical and material world through rigorous observation and experimentation. This knowledge pertains to understanding the structure and behavior of the natural and physical universe. Newtonian Physics is a central pillar of this discourse, which has significantly shaped the scientific perspective on the nature of matter and the universe. In this paradigm, the majority of scientists believe that the universe is essentially mechanical. Matter is understood as being composed of cells and atoms, and it's through our observation and intervention that we interact with and influence the universe.

One of the foundational tenets of science is that its knowledge base consists of ideas and theories that have been meticulously tested and proven. While there might occasionally be some ambiguity in experimental results, the power of the scientific method is such that we can replicate the results. This reproducibility lends significant credibility to scientific findings. Central to this method is a rigorous hypothesis formulation, testing, and relentless questioning process.

The scientific method isn't just a tool for scientists; it provides a framework for how we should process information and experiences in our daily lives. This approach has been instrumental in shaping our understanding of the world and ourselves. To further illustrate this,

I've included some renowned scientific experiments and findings that shed light on human nature and our relationship with our environment. As we delve into these, I urge you to critically analyze and question the information presented, testing our beliefs against the scrutiny of evidence.

One profound assertion is that our thoughts shape our reality. It is estimated that trillions of microorganisms inhabit the human body, relying on us for their existence. This symbiosis suggests that, in a way, we are their creators. Science has shown that matter, including ourselves, comprises atoms. These atoms consist of positively charged protons and negatively charged electrons. When in balance, they generate energy, much like how an electric plug powers an appliance. Nature inherently strives for this balance. However, our perceptions can skew our interpretation of natural events, such as perceiving a forest fire as sheer destruction, while in nature's view, it's a rejuvenating process.

Beyond the tangible physical world that we see, scientific experiments, like the famous Double-slit Experiment, reveal that matter exists as waves until observed. It is our act of observation that materializes the world around us. This suggests that our perceptions, beliefs, and collective consciousness play a pivotal role in shaping our reality.

A notable theoretical physicist, Dr. John Wheeler, proposed the Participatory Anthropic Principle, suggesting that reality necessitates an observer. His Delayed-choice Experiment further highlighted the intricate relationship between observation and the behavior of photons. Similarly, a cellular biologist, Dr. Bruce Lipton, found that our beliefs influence our cells. He noted that genes are merely blueprints, and the environment, shaped by our perceptions, determines cellular behavior.

The nature versus nurture debate, sparked by thinkers like Charles Darwin and Jean-Baptiste Lamarck, still rages on. However, there's a growing consensus that genetic inheritance and environmental factors play pivotal roles in an organism's development. An embryo's genes result from parental influences, but as a child grows, its environment, which includes parental beliefs, plays a significant role in its perceptions and understanding of the world.

Masaru Emoto's research proposed that human consciousness impacts the molecular structure of water. His experiments suggested that our environment, shaped by our perceptions, can be altered, reinforcing that we are the architects of our reality. Similarly, a former NASA physicist, Thomas Campbell, emphasized that a more extensive consciousness system aids our personal growth.

Our understanding that thoughts influence reality has profound implications. However, when we chase emotional desires, we often overlook this principle. As Newton's Third Law of Motion suggests, every action has an equal and opposite reaction. Thus, our desires and emotions inherently contain their counterforces. This understanding is pivotal in scientific explorations and should guide our introspection about our thoughts and actions.

The karmic principle resonates with this idea. Every emotional experience we pursue sets in motion its counter-experience, aiming for a balanced state. For instance, to truly comprehend love, one needs to have an understanding of its opposite. This interplay of emotions and experiences is a dance of creation and balance, underscoring the interconnectedness of all things.

Spirituality and Our Inner Quest

Spirituality represents a pursuit of higher consciousness with the intent to understand our divine nature and our connection to the universe. While other disciplines may seek similar goals, spiritual quests stand out due to their personal and individualistic nature. The insights garnered aren't from external doctrines but from inner reflections and unique experiences. The hallmark of a spiritual journey lies in the seeker's aim to find fulfillment in their current life rather than in an afterlife.

Spiritual practices span a wide range: New Age, Psychotherapy, hallucinogenic drugs, Wicca, Shamanism, breathwork, yoga, holistic medicine, and esoteric teachings like Gnosticism, Sufism, and Kabbalah, to name a few. Essentially, they encompass any activity undertaken to awaken or enlighten oneself during one's lifetime.

Pierre Teilhard de Chardin, a French philosopher, beautifully encapsulated this when he said, “We are not human beings having a spiritual experience; we are spiritual beings having a human experience.”

The Essence of Our Being

So, who are we fundamentally, and what does it mean to be a ‘spiritual being’? A rich narrative rooted in the depths of esoteric Hindu mythology offers profound insights into these existential questions.

According to the tale, Brahma, the cosmic creator in Hindu belief, brought the universe into existence. However, his divine status barred him from fully experiencing the creation he had shaped. To address this, he manifested Maya, the Goddess of Illusion. Through her, Brahma gave life to every creature, but even then, he remained a distant observer, unable to engage with the unfolding drama of life. Maya, in her wisdom, proposed a solution: she imbued every human with a fragment of Brahma’s essence. Oblivious to the divine spark within, humans wander through the world, engaging in the intricate play of life, the grand drama set in motion by Maya and Brahma.

The true essence of our existence, as this tale suggests, is the journey towards realizing this inner divinity. It’s an awakening to the understanding that we are all interconnected, each of us a vital part of a larger, divine whole. This realization is not just an acknowledgment of our shared humanity but a recognition of our collective identity as fragments of a greater cosmic entity.

The illusion of separateness, perpetuated by our ego, keeps us anchored in this reality. Our ego, acting as Maya within our psyche, ensures we’re engrossed in life’s drama. To truly engage, we need boundaries, limitations, and attachments. If we were fully aware of our divine nature, our interactions would be bereft of depth, making life monotonous. Our egos, while varied, serve a common goal: to keep us entrenched in the illusion. Yet, the ultimate purpose is transcendence, recognizing our innate divinity.

The narrative of Brahma and Maya invites us to contemplate the divine spark within each of us, proposing that we are far more than mere physical beings; we are spiritual entities enmeshed in a cosmic play. This understanding brings forth the question: If we carry a fragment of the divine, how is this essence reflected in the life we lead and the bodies we inhabit?

Our Bodies: Mirrors of the Soul

Our physical form is the vessel that sails the seas of this grand illusion, an avatar that embodies the fragment of Brahma within. It is through this vessel that we experience the world, and just as the soul yearns for realization and transcendence, our bodies communicate deeper truths through the language of sensation and emotion. They are not just biological constructs but mirrors reflecting our inner emotional states and spiritual balance.

When we experience discomfort or dis-ease within our bodies, it is often a manifestation of an inner disturbance, an echo of the drama orchestrated by Maya that plays out within the depths of our psyche. A sore throat might not merely be a physical ailment but a symbol of stifled expression, and heartache may not solely signify a medical condition but might also indicate a deeper emotional blockage.

It is through the acknowledgment of these signals and the inward journey that we approach healing. The physical symptoms are clues, urging us to explore the unresolved issues that we carry within our energy fields. Whether through energy healing that aligns with our spiritual being, medical interventions for our physical needs, or psychotherapy that bridges the two, we possess the incredible potential to harmonize our being. Our minds, powerful beyond measure, hold the keys to both the genesis and the resolution of our ailments, echoing the duality of Maya, the illusion and the enlightenment wrapped within our human experience.

Humans are often defined by physicality, but our bodies are more than biological entities. They're metaphors for our stored emotions and unresolved issues. Discomfort in specific body parts can symbolize emotional disturbances. For instance, a sore throat might suggest communication barriers, while heart discomfort could denote suppressed feelings.

Every experience, by nature, is emotion-neutral. However, our perceptions infuse emotions, creating imbalances. When these imbalances persist, they lodge within our energy fields, leading to discomfort. True healing comes from within through energy healing, medical intervention, or psychotherapy. Our minds wield the power to both ail and heal.

When a SCUBA diver experiences hypoxia, a condition of oxygen deprivation underwater, the immediate solution is to reintroduce oxygen to restore balance to the body. This process of addressing the imbalance is crucial for the diver's survival and well-being. Drawing a parallel from this, in our emotional and spiritual lives, we often find ourselves deprived or overwhelmed by certain emotions due to our deep investments in various life experiences. Just as a diver needs oxygen to restore physical balance, we need to find ways to release or manage our emotional investments to achieve emotional and spiritual equilibrium.

In life, we frequently become entangled in our emotional responses to different situations, forgetting that experiences are transient and ever-changing. These strong attachments and reactions can create imbalances in our emotional and spiritual well-being. For example, holding onto anger, grief, or even excessive joy can disrupt our inner peace and cloud our judgment, much like how hypoxia impairs a diver's ability to think clearly and function underwater.

To rectify these imbalances and promote spiritual growth, we need to practice letting go of these emotional attachments. This doesn't mean becoming emotionless or indifferent but rather learning to experience emotions without letting them dominate our lives. It involves understanding the temporary nature of experiences and emotions and developing the ability to observe them without getting caught up in them. By doing so, just like the diver who restores oxygen balance, we can achieve a state of emotional and spiritual balance, leading to a more centered, peaceful, and enlightened existence.

Dis-Ease: The Physical Manifestation of Imbalance

"Dis-Ease: The Physical Manifestation of Imbalance" refers to the concept that our body, much like a precisely calibrated instrument, is sensitive to the energies we carry within us. It suggests that the body can act as a repository for the energy created by our emotions and experiences, especially those that are unresolved or unreconciled.

When we experience emotions such as anger, grief, or stress and fail to process or release them effectively, they can become trapped within our bodies. This trapped emotional energy can disrupt the body's natural balance and flow. Over time, these unresolved emotional energies can accumulate, creating blockages and imbalances in the body's energy system.

These blockages can manifest physically in various ways, often as discomfort, pain, or illness. The term 'dis-ease' is used to describe this phenomenon, highlighting that it's not just a physical disease in the conventional sense but a state of unease or imbalance originating from emotional and energetic disturbances. This perspective aligns with many holistic health philosophies that view the mind, body, and spirit as interconnected and interdependent.

Our body often communicates these imbalances to us through symptoms. For instance, chronic stress might manifest as headaches, digestive issues, or muscle tension. By paying attention to these signals, we can gain insights into our emotional state and the unresolved issues that might be affecting our physical health.

Addressing these imbalances often requires more than just treating the physical symptoms. It involves delving into the emotional aspects underlying the physical manifestations. This might include practices such as meditation, counseling, or other forms of emotional release work. By confronting and processing these trapped emotions, we can begin to dissolve the blockages, allowing the body to return to its natural state of balance and health.

This approach to health and well-being underscores the importance of considering both the physical and emotional aspects of our lives. It suggests that profound healing, both physical and spiritual, can be achieved by recognizing and addressing the emotional roots of our physical dis-ease, leading to a more harmonious and balanced state of being.

Unveiling the Mask: Understanding Our Divine Essence in the Earthly Journey

The elusive question of 'why are we here?' may not have a definitive answer. Yet, through my understanding, I've often contemplated the purpose of our incarnation into this physical realm. Why would beings endowed with such supreme, infinite potential, masters of creation, opt for the human experience? While our earthly existence might seem like an illusion in the cosmic context, it offers a spectrum of emotions and experiences that are unique and otherwise unattainable. It's in this realm that we experience the complexity of love, hate, joy, sorrow, friendships, fear, bravery, wellness, ailment, birth, and death. This intricate reality serves as a stage, a canvas of limitations against the expanse of our eternal existence, prompting our evolution and recognition of our inherent divinity. To truly understand this, we incarnate as sentient beings, equipped with intellect and reason, to amass experiences, all aimed at remembering our unity with the divine, a truth often veiled by the nature of our earthly journey.

Upon our arrival in this world, we innately sense our divine origin, yet we adopt a metaphorical mask to navigate this realm effectively. This mask becomes our means to experience the vast array of emotions and states we encounter. Over time, many of us forget that this mask is not our true self. However, to fully realize our divine essence and cultivate a harmonious existence, it's crucial to recognize and remain conscious of this mask. Such awareness fosters balanced interactions, guiding us through life without succumbing to imbalances or distortions.

The concept of reincarnation is often embraced to explain our journey towards self-awareness, suggesting a path through multiple lifetimes of accumulated experiences leading to enlightenment. However, belief in past lives isn't necessary. The linear concept of time is misleading. We might access experiences that appear anchored in a distant past or future, but these are merely portals into the vast collective consciousness.

Every moment of existence, every subtlety, is ours to explore in the now. Embracing this truth, recognize that every aspect of your life, every interaction and challenge, carries profound significance and lessons. This includes your career, relationships, possessions, and family. The elements of your life that challenge or disconcert you are opportunities for transcendence. Your external world reflects your internal state. To harmonize with your true nature, you must let go of these perceptions, release attachments and misconceptions, and immerse yourself in the radiant essence of your true being."

Inner Alchemy: Self-Realization and the Power Within and Embracing Inner Knowledge

Transformation is an innate journey, a path unique to each of us. It commences with introspection, questioning the very core of our learned experiences and beliefs. As we delve deeper, we often find that the wisdom we seek and the truths we yearn to understand have always been accessible, nestled within the recesses of our being. The answers to life's grand questions are ours by birthright; our challenge lies in the recognition and acceptance of this knowledge.

Embarking on this journey doesn't require grand gestures or pilgrimages in search of enlightenment. It doesn't necessitate guidance from spiritual gurus or adherence to rigorous practices like meditation, yoga, or nature retreats, though they may serve as valuable tools for some. The essence of transformation lies in the courage to confront and question our beliefs, to shed the layers of stringent beliefs and preconceived notions, and to boldly embrace the innate wisdom that resides within each of us.

The Paradox of Change: Sculpting the Self

The paradoxical truth captured in the statement, 'You believe that you need to change, but the instrument you are using to change is the instrument you are trying to change,' illuminates the complexity of personal transformation. We are both the sculptor and the marble, the artist and the canvas. The very self that seeks transformation is, simultaneously, the means through which change must occur. This reveals a profound truth: the barrier to our transformation is often ourselves.

Our greatest obstacle is the recognition of this fact. Once we understand that we are the architects of our destiny, the creators of our reality, the path to self-realization unfolds before us with clarity. Seeking external validation or established pathways can lead us astray, further from the realization that we are, in essence, the embodiment of the nirvana we seek. It is not in the seeking but in the understanding and embracing of our authentic selves, without reliance on external affirmations, that true transformation occurs. We must become the change we wish to see, using our inherent self as both the tool and the material for our personal evolution.

Breaking Free: The Journey from Blind Faith to Personal Enlightenment

Conflict emerges when we latch onto desires or become entrenched in experiences, inhibiting our ability to move forward. Both desire and attachment are potent sources of discord. Similarly, blind allegiance to unscrutinized beliefs can foster internal turmoil.

This speaks to the dangers of adopting beliefs without personal reflection or understanding: essentially, having blind faith. This kind of faith means accepting ideas and paths laid out by others, which can lead us away from our true selves and potentially down a path that doesn't serve our personal growth or reality. Thomas Campbell, a physicist and author, argues that truth should not be accepted just because a majority believes it or because it comes from an authority. Truth must be personally experienced and validated.

The story of the circus elephant is used to illustrate how beliefs can limit us. The elephant, conditioned from a young age to believe it cannot escape because it was restrained by a small chain, continues to believe this even when it has grown strong enough to break free. Similarly, we can become trapped by beliefs that we've accepted from others, beliefs that may not actually reflect our true potential or capabilities.

By challenging and redefining societal norms, much like ice swimmers who brave frigid waters despite common beliefs about human limitations, we demonstrate the ability to overcome perceived barriers. This approach calls for an objective analysis of the world and our experiences within it. Recognizing that each experience is either a lesson to be learned or simply an event in our lives allows us to develop a deeper understanding and balance.

To truly live freely, it's necessary to differentiate between the roles we assume in society and who we really are. Our beliefs can act like masks, obscuring our view of reality if we become too attached to them. Understanding that every event in our life has a purpose and that there's a certain designed synchronicity to our experiences encourages us to look for the deeper meaning in each event without jumping to conclusions based on our preconceived notions.

In essence, this is a call to personal empowerment and enlightenment through self-discovery, critical thinking, and the courage to confront and question the beliefs we hold. By doing so, we can align our lives with our authentic selves and live in a state of true freedom and harmony.

The Power of Belief: Shaping Our Reality

Our belief system shapes our reality as exemplified by the nocebo effect; our convictions manifest physically, whether grounded in reality or not. Trust should not be unquestionably given based on perceived authority. Recognizing our innate power and the pivotal role of our minds can shift our realities. The narratives we tell ourselves, be it blaming genetics or external factors, shape our experiences. But by embracing a new perspective and releasing emotional burdens, we can unearth the divine purpose of our existence.

The Bhagavad Gita encapsulates the essence of belief, asserting that our faith molds us. The tale of Tarzan illustrates how deeply entrenched beliefs shape actions. Though a product of our environment, culture, and experiences, we have the power to transcend these constraints. Our self-perception is pivotal; a shift in this perception can alter our entire world. Embracing our true essence ensures experiences align with our joy. But challenges will arise, especially when unlearned lessons linger. Ultimately, the stories we tell ourselves determine our realities. Believe you're confined, and you will remain so. Embrace your limitless potential, and watch as boundaries dissolve.

The Emotional Landscape: Techniques for Release

The journey towards self-realization requires freeing ourselves from past burdens and outdated beliefs. The essence of this transformative process is to shed what no longer serves us. I'll introduce you to an exercise derived from Robert Scheinfeld's technique for emotional release. This is your moment; immerse yourself fully in this exercise and witness a shift in your perspective.

1. Recall and Relive: Begin by searching your mind for a memorable experience. Whether it is a joyful or sorrowful memory, the nature of it is irrelevant.
2. Ground Yourself: Before delving deep, remember that the emotions tied to this experience are mere illusions.
3. Vivid Visualization: Envelop yourself in the memory. Observe the colors, sounds, and sensations it evokes. Identify and dissect the emotions it stirs within.
4. Embrace the Emotion: Allow yourself to completely feel the emotion, naming it honestly and recognizing its peak.
5. Empower Yourself: Reclaim the energy you invested in this emotion.
6. Release and Appreciate: Let go of the emotion and be grateful for the wisdom it imparted.

The Power of Observation

The technique above is a step towards mastering the art of observation, a transformative tool that enables us to experience life's rich tapestry without being ensnared by our emotions. Observing is about understanding the intricate layers of each moment, indulging in emotion while maintaining the ability to detach from it as needed. This art of observation gives us the freedom of choice.

Consider a scenario where you find yourself in disagreement during a discussion. This disagreement is rooted in emotion-laden judgments. By choosing to listen rather than contest, you practice observation. Each unique perspective is a thread in the broader narrative of human experience. If you choose to respond, it is an opportunity to nurture or transcend your ego. A seasoned observer evaluates without attachment, understanding that each view contributes to a comprehensive understanding of the subject and, consequently, to a richer self-awareness.

This practice of observation is a stepping stone to achieving the Natural State, harmony in its purest form. In this state, you accept the inevitability of conflict, striving for balance. Many are trapped by their emotions, perceiving them as the ultimate reality. The key is to see through this deception, to feel emotions, release them, and to be grateful for their existence and the lessons they impart. In recognizing the restraints of societal expectations, we come to see life not as a series of entrapments but as a grandiose performance, an enchanting illusion to be observed, learned from, and, ultimately, appreciated in its full glory.

Life is a tapestry of diverse experiences and emotions. While emotions are an intrinsic part of being human, mastering the art of observation can be transformative. Being a conscious observer means living life and understanding the deeper layers that form every moment. It grants us the power to indulge in an emotion and just as swiftly disconnect from it, providing the freedom of choice.

Imagine engaging in a discussion where you disagree with someone. Recognize that your disagreement is an emotion-laden judgment. Instead of contesting, listen. Understand that every perspective is unique and merely a chapter in the larger narrative. If you opt to respond, be aware that you're nurturing your ego. A true observer discerns without judgment, realizing that every opinion provides a fuller understanding of the subject and, in turn, oneself. Practice this observation; over time, it will seamlessly integrate into your natural demeanor, reducing conflicts and enhancing understanding.

The Natural State is harmony in its truest form - a realm devoid of conflicts and desires. In this state, dualities merge, revealing the inherent beauty in all spectrums of existence. To thrive in the Natural State means acknowledging inevitable conflicts and seeking equilibrium. Many are ensnared by emotions, mistaking them for reality, but the key lies in discerning emotions, releasing them, and expressing gratitude for their teachings. Recognize the chains of societal norms and remember life is but a grand spectacle, an alluring mirage.

The essence of our existence, connection with the divine, and purpose in this vast cosmos have been explored. The realization that we are fragments of the supreme, intertwined by collective consciousness, is profound. The reality we know is crafted by thoughts, and with conscious intent, we wield the power to shape our future.

Embrace the observer within, navigate life with intention, and harmonize with your true nature. As we evolve, the intricacies of this cosmic play become evident, revealing how emotions anchor us to experiences. Whether you choose to stay in the dream or awaken to a new reality, remember barriers are self-imposed.

The Hindu Trimurti (Brahma the Creator, Vishnu the Preserver, and Shiva the Destroyer) mirrors the cyclical nature of our beliefs, life, and even our world. Everything has its dawn, zenith, and eventual dusk.

In this ephemeral existence, cherish the reality you've sculpted.

PART TWO: The Preservation (Life)

In the steady rhythm of a pendulum's swing, we find a manifestation of the principle of action and reaction. Just as every swing has its counter-swing, every action reverberates with a reaction. We can liken this dance to the principle of karma. Closer to the pendulum's base, its arcs are grand and sweeping. Analogously, our youth is marked by impulsive, dramatic actions, often meeting with significant repercussions. But with age comes wisdom that teaches us the beauty of balance. With growing consciousness, our actions become measured, seeking equilibrium and harmony. In this state of perfect balance, akin to a pendulum at rest, we stand undisturbed by the ripples of karma, becoming tranquil observers of the reality we inhabit.

This pendulum perspective enlightens us about the profound impacts of our deeds. Outward displays of affection might sometimes hide an inner void, a longing for external validation to fill the chasm of self-worth. From our early years, trust is instilled in us: trust in parents, peers, mentors, and societal pillars. This trust, while comforting, often comes at the expense of our individuality, nudging us to fit predefined templates or risk alienation. While these molds might have once been evolutionary necessities, they frequently distance us from our innate intuitive sense, pushing us toward collective opinions.

Challenging entrenched norms might seem daunting and met with resistance, skepticism, and often mockery. Even sacred institutions like religions sometimes create an environment where questions and introspections are discouraged, where we place divine figures on pedestals, unapproachable and unattainable.

Such questioning, especially as one grows in self-awareness, can be isolating. A pervasive mindset emerges, reminiscent of crabs pulling each other down in a barrel, echoing the sentiment, "If it's beyond my reach, it should be beyond yours too." Yielding to this sentiment is a ticket to a life shadowed by regret.

The philosophical and spiritual concept of the "divine spark" within humans suggests that each person possesses an inherent but often obscured divinity, overshadowed by the ego. The notion here is that life is a stage, and humans are co-creators in its unfolding drama, with the universe playing a guiding role. This guidance is perceived through various means, such as coincidences, feelings of déjà vu, and sudden, deep realizations, which are seen as nudges toward realizing one's true purpose or calling in life.

The nature of divinity itself is often portrayed with human emotions in various religious and spiritual texts, leading to a paradox. The idea is that a truly divine entity, often considered perfect in many traditions, shouldn't possess human imperfections. This contradiction is highlighted by referring to Occam's Razor, a philosophical principle that suggests the simplest explanation is usually the correct one. In this context, it implies that the true nature of divinity might be a simple yet profound force that underpins reality rather than a complex, human-like deity.

Furthermore, it contrasts the human quest for meaning and a tangible connection with the divine against the backdrop of nature, which is described as existing freely and beautifully, unencumbered by human-imposed religious doctrines. It touches on the elusive nature of definitive proof of a deity that demands unwavering devotion, suggesting that such proof lies beyond the reach of religious scriptures and doctrines that claim to fully comprehend the divine. This perspective invites contemplation of spirituality and divinity as concepts that are perhaps broader and more mysterious than traditionally understood within the confines of organized religion.

Chapter 5 | Unlocking the Chains of Your Mind

The first four chapters established the terrain: we are biologically adaptable, collectively connected, spiritually integrated beings who carry the creative capacity described equally by religion, science, and spirituality. If Part One asked what we are made of, Part Two now asks a harder and more personal question: what is keeping us from being that fully?

"The mind is everything. What you think, you become." – Buddha

The complex tapestry of the human mind is woven with threads of potential, ambition, desires, and inhibitions. Yet, a prominent thread in this weave is the beliefs that often act as self-imposed shackles, restricting our movement and growth.

The Enslaved Mind: Origins and Impacts

Every belief system carves out its unique space in society. These systems build bridges and foster understanding when rooted in acceptance and tolerance. However, the line between respecting beliefs and becoming entrapped by them is thin.

The enslaved mind is a concept that captures our tendency to surrender to self-imposed beliefs and limitations. Its genesis lies in the unchecked ego that has evolved, placing undue emphasis on self-preservation, a trait essential for our ancestors' survival but potentially limiting in our current context.

As societies grew complex and intertwined, the collective consciousness began dictating terms, urging individuals to conform. While providing a sense of belonging, this conformity often eclipses individual thought and creativity, making us mere reflections of collective opinions.

Rising above societal labels, biases, and prejudices uncovers an underlying universal truth: our innate ability to love, empathize, and care. Thus, challenging and evolving our beliefs doesn't undermine them; it refines them, bringing us closer to profound truths beneath superficial differences.

What holds us back is fear.

Fear, often an intangible entity, plays a pivotal role in shaping our beliefs. Be it fear of the unknown, fear of rejection, or fear of judgment, these emotions anchor many of our convictions. Influential institutions, both religious and governmental, astutely employ this mechanism. They sow seeds of fear, ensuring conformity and allegiance. Modern societies, emphasizing stereotypes and divisive narratives, further amplify these fears. In contrast, certain philosophies, like Zen Buddhism, advocate a different approach, emphasizing inner divinity and interconnectedness.

Embracing the Inner Self: The Path Forward

For many, the familiar comfort of established beliefs is too tempting to abandon. However, a world teeming with potential is buried beneath layers of conditioning and societal expectations. This inward journey is akin to navigating a labyrinth, fraught with challenges and inner demons. Memories and unresolved emotions, if left unaddressed, can hamper our quest for enlightenment. To truly experience freedom, one must confront these shadows, understand them, and eventually let them go.

Leaders and institutions, wielding influence, craft narratives that reinforce their dominion. An Enslaved Mind, overwhelmed by external noise, struggles to see beyond these crafted narratives. However, the road to liberation begins with introspection, questioning, and challenging these deep-rooted beliefs.

It's imperative to remember that fear is essentially a construct of the mind, a tool skillfully wielded to ensure compliance and conformity. Recognizing this illusion shatters the very foundation of many of our inhibitions, enabling us to embark on a transformative journey of self-discovery.

By challenging our beliefs and confronting our fears, we unlock our potential and rediscover the boundless wonders of our minds. As we peel away the layers of fear and dismantle the chains of conditioned thought, we pave the way for the birth of new perspectives. This metamorphosis is not just an end but a beginning, where the cleared space of our unshackled minds becomes fertile ground for the seeds of imagination. No longer confined by the 'what is,' we are free to explore the 'what could be.'

Embracing the infinite playground of our imagination, we allow our once-dormant dreams to blossom into vibrant expressions of our innate potential. Here, in this sanctuary of liberated thought, we find the courage to paint our future with the bold strokes of visionary ideas and limitless horizons. Thus, unfettered by the ghosts of our past, we step into the realm of imagination, the key to unlocking the infinite possibilities that await.

Imagination: The Key to Infinite Horizons

Imagination stands as the key to unlocking infinite horizons. This ethereal bridge transcends the gap between the tangible world of our current experiences and the intangible realm of possibilities yet to materialize. This cognitive ability, often overshadowed by the immediate demands of everyday life, is the engine of human progress, the silent power behind our most significant achievements. It is the force that has transformed the whispers of our dreams into the concrete reality we live in today.

Our days were awash with the colors of dreams and unbridled creativity as children. Our young minds knew no bounds, as every thought sparkled with the potential of 'what could be.' We built castles in the air and imagined ourselves in the farthest reaches of space and the deepest depths of the oceans. This luminous intensity of childhood imagination serves as a poignant reminder of a time when the horizon of possibility stretched out infinitely before us.

However, the path to adulthood often brings with it a dimming of this inner light. The vibrancy of our imagination can fade beneath the weight of practical responsibilities and societal norms. Yet, despite this, history is replete with visionaries who have harnessed the power of imagination to catalyze change and innovation. These individuals dreamed of the unseen, from the audacious idea of connecting continents to the realization of global communication through technology, demonstrating the indomitable will of the human spirit to bring forth the once inconceivable into our lived experience.

The line between imagination and perceived reality is not always clear-cut. For those experiencing conditions like schizophrenia, where the mind may present a reality starkly different from the consensus, the very concept of reality becomes fluid. Such conditions invite us to reconsider the rigid frameworks we often use to define our world. They are a testament to the expansive nature of human perception and the complex interplay between our inner and outer worlds.

Imagination is the compass that guides us through the uncharted territories of innovation and creation. By cherishing and cultivating this innate capacity, we unlock doors to realms never before explored. It encourages us to envision the world not just as it is but as it could be. When we embrace the full spectrum of our imaginative faculties, we tune into new frequencies of the universe, broadening our collective consciousness. In the symphony of human thought, what we conceive in our minds has the potential to manifest into our reality, reshaping our existence and the fabric of society. Our ability to dream, therefore, is not merely an escape from reality but a conduit to shape it, a tool to sculpt our future and redefine the boundaries of our world.

The Universe and Our Thoughts: A Cosmic Dance

The Universe's responsiveness to our thoughts is interwoven with mysticism and metaphysical principles, notably within the Law of Attraction. This law suggests a universe in perpetual engagement with our deepest wishes and thoughts, resonating with the energies we emit.

At its core, the Law of Attraction champions the profound impact of belief, our conviction that our desires are not mere figments but preludes to reality. Our conscious and subconscious thoughts are believed to mold our experiences, drawing to us events and scenarios that echo our internal state. According to this law, a positive mindset is a magnet for favorable outcomes, just as negative thinking may perpetuate undesirable situations.

Natural human emotions like doubt and fear, while inevitable, are considered distractions within this framework. They are mere shadows when compared to the brightness of firm belief. The strength of our faith can illuminate our path, directing the universe to align with our aspirations. This isn't just symbolic; the Law of Attraction purports that such faith can tangibly influence our life's direction.

Mindfulness is thus imperative, urging us to be vigilant of our mental and emotional outputs. By doing so, we leverage the power of our convictions to craft our destiny. The Law of Attraction is essentially an introspective odyssey, connecting our inner vibrations with the cosmic tapestry.

Mirroring this mystical law, physics introduces "constructive interference," where waves in sync amplify their combined energy. This can be an allegory for human interactions, where matching energetic vibrations can elevate our collective presence.

The Spane Scale research contributes a fascinating dimension to this conversation by positing that authenticity, the act of being our true selves, resonates within us at the highest frequency. This concept suggests that when we embrace and express our genuine nature, our energy becomes undiluted, powerful, and coherent. This is comparable to the focused beam of a laser, which is a concentrated form of light known for its precision and power. The metaphor implies that just as a laser beam channels light in a single, potent direction, being authentic channels our personal energy in a more impactful and clear manner.

In contrast, the presence of fear can significantly disrupt this harmonious state. Fear is likened here to destructive interference, a concept from physics where overlapping waves that are out of phase with each other lead to a decrease in overall amplitude. In a similar vein, fear introduces a kind of emotional and psychological interference. It clashes with our authentic selves, lowering our vibrational state and introducing chaos and confusion. This process can be visualized as waves of energy that, instead of aligning and strengthening each other, collide and weaken the overall energy field. The clarity and strength with which we project ourselves are thus diminished, muddied by the dissonance fear creates.

This expanded view highlights a compelling interplay between our inner state and the energy we project. It underscores the transformative power of authenticity and the disruptive nature of fear, suggesting that our emotional and psychological states are not just internal experiences but also resonate outwardly, affecting the energy we emit and interact with.

Synthesizing these notions, we see a human experience deeply entrenched in energetic dynamics. Authenticity and intentionality in alignment with our true nature enhance our vibrational impact. The Law of Attraction, therefore, transcends mysticism, finding parallel in the concrete principles of physics, reminding us of the imperative to cultivate positive, genuine interactions to amplify our vibrational essence in the universe.

The concept of the Universe responding to our thoughts is a tapestry woven with threads of mysticism and metaphysics, central to the esoteric Law of Attraction. This principle posits that the cosmos itself is in a continuous, dynamic dance with our innermost desires and thoughts, vibrating at frequencies that align with the energy we emit through our mental and emotional states. In the intricate dance of the universe, where the Law of Attraction suggests a symbiotic relationship between our innermost energies and the cosmos, we find a bridge to the realm of personal wellness. Just as we have seen how a positive mindset and authenticity can amplify our energetic presence and influence our reality, this same power of belief extends into the domain of our physical health.

Transitioning from the cosmic interplay of energies to the intimate corridors of our own being, we approach the concept of wellness not merely as the absence of illness but as a dynamic state of being influenced by the mind. Here, the potent vibrations of thought and emotion play a crucial role, akin to how constructive interference amplifies waves in physics. Our mental state, replete with beliefs, attitudes, and perceptions, can profoundly shape our physical condition.

The Spane Scale research illuminates this connection, indicating that authenticity, living in alignment with our true selves, generates the highest energy frequency within us. When this authenticity is compromised by fear, our vibrational state is lowered, muddying our self-expression and, by extension, potentially affecting our physical wellness. The mind's influence on the body is thus not a mere metaphor but a tangible force, where thoughts saturated with positivity or negativity can manifest as wellness or ailment.

The Mind's Power Over Wellness: Beyond Being *Broken*

The concept of the mind's power over wellness extends this dialogue, offering a perspective that challenges the notion of being *broken*. Depending on our mental narratives, it underlines the mind's profound ability to invite wellness or sickness. Our interpretations and reactions to life's experiences can seed our bodies with the fruits of health or the symptoms of distress.

To bridge the cosmic principles of the Law of Attraction with the personal power over wellness, we must see our mind as the fertile ground from which our physical experiences sprout. By cultivating a garden of positive thoughts and emotional states, we can nurture a body that thrives in health and vitality. This connection is pivotal in understanding how our perceptions, consciously directed and harmonized with our authentic selves, can weave the tapestry of our overall well-being.

Often, we hear the sentiment, "You may be broken, but you are not sick." This statement touches on the profound connection between our mind and physical well-being. Understanding this bond is pivotal in recognizing how our mental state can influence our health and well-being.

Every experience, sensation, or ailment our body undergoes can be traced back to the mind's perception. Our mind interprets, assesses, and ultimately decides how we react to external stimuli. If we are engulfed in a mindset that we're unwell, the body can manifest these thoughts into actual symptoms. Conversely, a positive, harmonious mind can create an environment for wellness. Think of the mind as a garden; nurturing it with positive thoughts and emotions will yield a healthy body.

When we expose ourselves consistently to negative influences or environments, our minds will inevitably absorb some of this negativity. Over time, this can develop into a belief system that could compromise our well-being. In essence, our internal reality mirrors our external environment.

A striking example of the mind's influence over the body can be found in Jolo, West Virginia. The Church of the Lord Jesus has followers who, as a testament to their unwavering faith, consume Strychnine from venomous snakes. Most would deem this act lethal, yet their profound faith shields them. Their mind, so deeply entrenched in belief, acts as a barrier against the poison. This example may be extreme, but it demonstrates the potential power of unwavering belief.

The placebo and nocebo effects also underscore the mind's potency. A placebo can lead to genuine healing, even if it's merely a sugar pill, while a nocebo can induce real symptoms out of mere suggestion. Both phenomena showcase how robust our beliefs can be, protecting or harming us.

Reconciling Belief with Practice: The Holistic Renaissance in Modern Western Medicine

The journey of Western medicine, from its roots steeped in the sanctity of religious and spiritual tradition to its current empirical and symptom-focused paradigm, intersects intriguingly with Adrian Cooper's insights in *Our Ultimate Reality*. Cooper explores the profound influence of belief systems on healing, suggesting that health transcends the physical and taps into the metaphysical realm shaped by our beliefs. This perspective echoes the historical holistic approach to health, where the spiritual and physical were inseparable, and healing was as much an art as a science.

Ancient cultures laid the foundation for what would evolve into Western medicine, viewing healers as conduits of divine power integrating rituals with practical care. This paradigm persisted through various epochs, with institutions like the temples of Asclepius and later Christian monasteries preserving the sanctity of holistic care. However, as the Renaissance ushered in a new age of anatomical discovery and the Enlightenment championed scientific inquiry, the lens through which medicine was practiced narrowed, focusing more on the body as a machine with problems to be fixed rather than a being to be healed.

The subsequent centuries saw an intensification of this approach, as germ theory and pharmaceutical advances prioritized the identification and treatment of symptoms, often sidelining the patient's emotional and spiritual context. Yet, as Cooper suggests, our internal belief systems are critical in directing the flow of our healing energies. The positive mindset that ancient healers implicitly understood is now finding resonance again in the contemporary resurgence of interest in integrative medicine, which seeks to meld the precision of modern science with the wisdom of holistic traditions.

Just as the mind's perceptions and beliefs were once integral to old healing practices, modern integrative medicine recognizes the mind-body connection as pivotal in the healing process. Cooper's assertion of an inner force of greatness capable of shaping our reality aligns with the growing understanding of health as the absence of disease and the presence of overall well-being. This recognition signals a return to a more balanced view, where the spiritual and emotional states are acknowledged as powerful influencers of physical health.

Merging these viewpoints, we see a comprehensive narrative: recognizing that our beliefs are potent forces that can promote or hinder healing. In its recognition of this power, Western medicine is beginning to embrace the holistic principles that honor the interplay of mind, body, and spirit. This shift represents a full circle in medical philosophy, a return to an understanding of health that is as ancient as it is urgently contemporary. By acknowledging the limitations of a purely symptom-driven model and re-incorporating the holistic wisdom of the past, we open the door to a more profound and effective form of healing that honors the entirety of the human experience.

Chapter 6 | The Spectrum of Awareness

"The real voyage of discovery consists not in seeking new landscapes, but in having new eyes." – Marcel Proust

As we traverse the spectrum of awareness, understanding the role of selective attention as our mind's spotlight, we come to appreciate its ability to filter and focus our experiences. This spotlight enables us to engage deeply with specific elements of our environment, such as the richness of a conversation, while relegating others to the background. Yet, beyond this selective focus lies a broader, more inclusive state of consciousness, a heightened awareness encompassing the full tapestry of sensory input and their emotional resonance.

The transition from a narrow beam to a broader glow of awareness is not automatic; it is a deliberate expansion cultivated through practices such as meditation and mindfulness. As we hone this ability, we begin to notice the immediate exchanges and the subtle textures of our environment: the play of light, the undertones of sound, and the emotional ambiance that pervades our space.

Within this vastness, emotions stand as powerful forces, coloring our perception and guiding our attention, often subliminally. They are the undercurrents that add depth and dimension to our awareness. Just as selective attention can zoom in on particular aspects of our environment, our emotions can filter this awareness, acting as prisms through which we interpret our world. Joy and optimism can widen our lens, inviting us to perceive our surroundings with greater receptivity and vibrancy. Conversely, when negative emotions grip us, our awareness can constrict, casting a pall over our perceptions and making the world appear less inviting.

Thus, as we seek to navigate between focused attention and broadened awareness, we must also consider the emotional dimension that interplays with our conscious experience. Our emotions can subtly influence our selective attention, intertwining with it to shape the narrative of our experiences. This emotional dimension makes our awareness richly textured, providing a backdrop against which we interpret the significance of a gesture or the meaning of a melody. Recognizing this intricate dance between our selective focus, the breadth of our awareness, and the emotional hues that tint it allows us to fully engage with the present, enriching our journey through life's grand narrative.

The Emotional Dimension of Awareness

Amidst the vastness of awareness, emotions hold a distinctive place. They serve as narrators and navigators, shaping and directing our conscious journey. Emotions are the silent currents, often steering our perceptions and responses, frequently beneath our conscious radar.

While centered on tasks or dialogues, selective attention constantly intermingles with our emotional states. A surge of happiness or a shadow of annoyance doesn't exist in a vacuum. They blend with our attention, influencing our interpretation of situations and surroundings.

Consider emotions as prisms. Our awareness broadens in states of joy or optimism, making us receptive to uplifting stimuli. Everything appears brighter; mundane details shimmer with newfound significance. However, when ensnared by negative emotions, our awareness often narrows, and the world seems more muted, even hostile.

These emotional layers render our experiences multifaceted. A casual gesture, colored by our emotional lens, can be perceived as a sign of affection or an intrusion. A familiar melody can evoke diverse emotions based on our current mood.

Being in tune with our emotional terrains is paramount for a holistic understanding of awareness. Recognizing the interplay of feelings and external stimuli empowers us to gauge whether our perceptions are objective or clouded by transient emotions.

Cultivating emotional intelligence involves developing a deep understanding of one's emotions and the emotions of others and the ability to manage and navigate these emotions effectively. It is the process of becoming acutely aware of how our feelings influence our thoughts and actions and how they can impact those around us. The potential for introspective depth is magnified when paired with mindfulness meditation, a practice that encourages present-moment awareness and acceptance.

Mindfulness meditation teaches us to observe our thoughts and feelings without judgment or immediate reaction. Through regular practice, we learn to recognize the ebb and flow of our emotions and the subtle ways they color our perception of the world. This heightened awareness allows us to pause and reflect rather than being swept away by our immediate emotional responses. It trains the mind to notice the present moment in all its fullness, fostering an attentiveness that can discern even the most nuanced emotional shifts.

With emotional intelligence, we take this awareness a step further by recognizing our emotions and understanding their origins and their influence on our behavior. This involves a continuous process of self-assessment and self-regulation. By applying the principles of mindfulness to our emotional lives, we become adept at identifying why we feel a certain way and how these feelings affect our interactions with others and our overall approach to situations.

As we sharpen these skills, we can more effectively manage our emotional responses, choosing actions that align with our values and goals rather than being reactive. For example, in a heated discussion, an emotionally intelligent and mindful individual would be able to recognize the rise of anger, understand its triggers, and choose a course of action that maintains constructive dialogue rather than escalating the conflict.

Combining emotional intelligence and mindfulness meditation leads to a balanced and insightful engagement with our environment. We become capable of responding to life's challenges with composure and clarity. This balanced approach not only enhances our well-being but also positively affects our relationships, making interactions more empathetic and productive. In essence, the practice of these disciplines fosters a holistic awareness that equips us to navigate the complexities of our emotional landscapes with grace and wisdom.

Emotions are the vibrant hues that paint our canvas of awareness. They embellish, guide, and occasionally mislead our perceptions. By acknowledging and assimilating this emotional dimension, we transform our awareness from a mere passive observance to an active, insightful exploration of the intricate dance between the external world and our inner psyche.

Carl Gustav Jung and the Collective Unconscious

Carl Gustav Jung, a pioneering Swiss psychiatrist and psychoanalyst, founded Analytical Psychology and introduced concepts that profoundly impacted our understanding of the human psyche. A cornerstone of his work is the notion of the collective unconscious, a universal layer of the unconscious mind not shaped by personal experience but shared across humanity. It is a reservoir of ancestral memories, symbols, and archetypes inherited from the shared experiences of our ancestors.

Archetypes, universally recognized symbols and themes, emerge from the collective unconscious and pervade our myths, dreams, and rituals. They are recurrent motifs that serve as blueprints for understanding shared human experiences and drive our reactions to life events.

Jung's *Red Book,* or *Liber Novus,* offers a profound insight into the depths of his engagement with the collective unconscious. Crafted over sixteen years, this book remained unpublished until 2009, long after Jung's death. A rich tapestry of his dreams, visions, and introspections, *The Red Book* is accompanied by evocative illustrations drawn by Jung himself. This work provides a raw, intimate window into the birth and evolution of his central theories.

Jung employs active imagination in *The Red Book*, a technique he devised to facilitate dialogue between one's conscious and unconscious realms. Through this, he confronts various symbolic entities, representing multifaceted aspects of his psyche. The text becomes a theater where Jung grapples with the universal dualities: light and shadow, individual and collective, and the terrestrial and the divine.

The Red Book is a testament to Jung's deep plunge into the vast ocean of collective unconscious, capturing the vibrant interplay of archetypes. It underscores the profound interconnectedness binding individual experiences with timeless, universal patterns. Jung's introspective journey magnifies the significance of self-awareness and introspection as pathways to understanding broader human experiences.

The "Shadow" in Jungian Psychology and Humanity's Inherent Capacity for Evil

At the heart of Carl Jung's analytical psychology lies the profound concept of the "shadow self," a term that captures those elements of our personality that remain unrecognized or unacknowledged by our conscious self. This shadow self is a repository not only of repressed desires, fears, and socially or personally unacceptable traits but also of latent talents and suppressed virtues. Jung's theory profoundly underscores the inherent capacity for evil within every individual, challenging the notion that malevolence is confined to a select few.

This concept of a universal potential for darkness within the human psyche is starkly mirrored in historical events, particularly in the rise of anti-Semitism in Nazi Germany under Adolf Hitler. Here, the amplification and exploitation of pre-existing anti-Semitic prejudices through Hitler's charismatic leadership and strategic propaganda demonstrate the real-world manifestation of the collective shadow. The Nazi regime's control over the media and the relentless spread of anti-Semitic ideology normalized these views, fostering an environment where hatred was not only accepted but encouraged. This historical example serves as a chilling illustration of how the unacknowledged and unexamined aspects of a collective psyche can lead to profound societal and moral breakdowns.

The tactics employed by Hitler and the Nazis (legal marginalization, psychological conditioning to dehumanize Jews, and exploiting group dynamics for conformity) resonate deeply with Jung's ideas about the shadow. They exemplify how a nation's collective shadow, filled with suppressed prejudices and fears, can erupt in catastrophic outcomes, such as the Holocaust.

Jung's call to acknowledge, confront, and integrate the shadow into our conscious lives thus becomes a critical undertaking, both personally and societally. It involves recognizing our shared capacity for evil and the ease with which propaganda can manipulate these shadow aspects. This self-awareness propels us towards continual self-reflection and ethical vigilance, emphasizing the need to understand and manage these darker impulses rather than succumbing to them.

Exploring and understanding our shadow self, both individually and collectively, is pivotal in navigating the complexities of human behavior and relationships. It's a journey toward aligning ourselves more closely with our ideals and contributing positively to the collective good. Jung's insights offer a potent reminder of the duality and complexity inherent in human nature, underscoring the importance of ethical integrity and empathy in our interactions with others and in our societal roles.

In summary, Jung's teachings on the shadow, reflecting both the negative and positive aspects of our hidden selves, serve as a critical lens through which we can understand human behavior, including the darker chapters of history. They highlight the necessity of confronting and integrating these shadow aspects to foster a more conscious, compassionate, and ethically aligned society.

Chapter 7 | Belief Is Everything

"Believe you can, and you're halfway there." –
Theodore Roosevelt

Belief, when distilled to its essence, is a powerful force that shapes our understanding of reality. While a standard dictionary might define belief as "a state or habit of mind in which trust or confidence is placed in some person or thing," it's much more profound than that simple definition suggests.

From the dawn of our consciousness, our beliefs are molded by a myriad of influences: parents, family, teachers, peers, and the wider community. This matrix of influences crafts our perspective on the world, dictating how we interpret and respond to our experiences. In many instances, these beliefs are deeply entrenched, discouraging questioning or skepticism. Religious, spiritual, and even some scientific convictions often fall into this category, shielded from doubt by a protective veil of tradition and authority.

In today's world, the immense progress in medical science has led society to place an unwavering faith in the capabilities of medicine, often to the extent of sidelining the tremendous power our minds hold over our well-being. While advancements in medicine are undeniably significant, it's equally crucial to recognize the mind's profound role in shaping our health and overall state. We're frequently conditioned to believe that when something feels off within us, the answer lies in an external remedy, whether it's a pill, procedure, or another person's expertise.

This external-seeking behavior is deeply rooted in the narratives we're surrounded by. We are frequently inundated with messages emphasizing our supposed flaws, suggesting that the path to healing lies outside ourselves. Yet, true healing and well-being often emerge when we trust ourselves and recognize that we might not be as inherently flawed as societal narratives suggest.

Moreover, as individuals, we often encase ourselves in invisible cages. These self-imposed limitations are products of societal expectations and norms. Whether it's the career we choose, the lifestyle we adopt, or even our health choices, we are bound by invisible threads of "shoulds" and "musts," primarily influenced by societal constructs.

Furthermore, while spiritual beliefs provide solace to many, an over-reliance on divine intervention can sometimes become a crutch. The belief that a higher power will step in and make things right can lead to passivity, allowing individuals to absolve themselves of responsibility for their actions and choices. It's essential to strike a balance between faith and active participation in one's life journey.

Beyond Passive Acceptance

Belief isn't just passive acceptance; it actively shapes our reality. The potency of belief is evident in the adage, "If you think you can't, you're right." The flip side? Belief can be a catalyst, turning improbable into possible. It's the foundation upon which dreams and endeavors are built. As the saying goes, to believe is to hope, but to have faith is to know.

Yet, beliefs can be double-edged. Some individuals and institutions, recognizing the magnetic pull of belief, might exploit this human tendency for their gain. When beliefs are dispensed from positions of authority, there's a risk that they morph into dogmas, fixed principles that discourage inquiry and promote adherence without understanding.

In *The Undiscovered Self*, Carl Jung eloquently encapsulated the essence of belief's role in shaping reality, suggesting that our consciousness, influenced by our beliefs, actively crafts our world. Our minds, powered by belief, are not just passive observers but active creators, molding matter and manifesting reality. When sufficiently energized, collective beliefs can have transformative effects on shared realities.

However, unexamined beliefs are akin to chains, limiting our potential and dictating our boundaries. The placebo and nocebo effects underscore the mind's capacity to transform belief into physical reality. This transformative power isn't always harnessed for our benefit. Individuals often internalize limiting beliefs, perceiving themselves as *broken* or *flawed*, trapped by societal expectations and judgments.

Political and religious institutions, aware of the power of beliefs, often weaponize it. They aim to retain control and suppress dissent by instilling fear and peddling dogmas. Those challenging the status quo are often ostracized, their voices stifled to maintain the sanctity of prevailing beliefs.

The journey to truth necessitates challenging these entrenched beliefs. Truth isn't about acquiring new knowledge but realizing what always was. Our self-imposed boundaries, born from unquestioned assumptions, are our self-made prisons. It's by questioning these beliefs that we can transcend these limitations.

Fear, often intertwined with belief, is an insidious force. While it serves a protective function, it can also trap us in cycles of avoidance and apprehension. Cultural narratives, such as the fear of death, are deeply ingrained, driving behaviors and decisions aimed at self-preservation. Yet, in obsessing over the end, do we truly live?

"The deeper and more emotionally charged our beliefs, the greater the changes we can make in both our bodies and reality itself." This quote by Michael Talbot from *The Holographic Universe* touches on the profound power of belief, especially when intertwined with strong emotions.

Let's break down this statement:

- **Deeper Beliefs:** When Talbot refers to deeper beliefs, he is discussing beliefs that are deeply ingrained in our psyche. These are not mere surface-level opinions or preferences but foundational convictions that shape our perception of ourselves and the world around us. Such beliefs often arise from long-held values, significant life experiences, or cultural teachings.
- **Emotionally Charged:** Emotion serves as an amplifier for belief. When a belief is tied to strong emotions, whether they be positive emotions like love and joy or negative ones like fear and anger, they become even more powerful. Emotions, by their very nature, are potent motivators for action and can significantly influence our behaviors, thoughts, and physiological responses.
- **Changes in Our Bodies:** Strong beliefs, especially those paired with potent emotions, can manifest physical changes

in our bodies. This is evident in phenomena like the placebo effect, where mere faith in a treatment's efficacy can lead to genuine physical improvements. Conversely, the nocebo effect demonstrates how negative expectations or beliefs can deteriorate health.

- **Changes in Reality Itself:** This part of the quote touches on subjective reality, the notion that our beliefs can shape the reality we experience. This doesn't mean that we can defy the laws of physics with mere thought, but our beliefs can profoundly influence our perceptions, interpretations, and experiences of reality. For instance, two individuals can experience the same event but interpret it differently based on their beliefs and emotional states.

Talbot's *The Holographic Universe* delves into the idea that the universe might be a hologram, a kind of projection from a deeper level of reality. In this context, the quote emphasizes that our beliefs and emotions are not just passive responses to the world but active contributors to the reality we experience. This notion underscores the human mind's immense potential and role in shaping personal and collective experiences.

Holographic Universe: A Conceptual Exploration

Michael Talbot's *The Holographic Universe* introduces a revolutionary notion: that our universe is akin to a vast, interconnected hologram. Drawing from quantum physics, Talbot builds on the understanding that every fragment of the universe mirrors the entirety of it, hinting at a profound level of interconnectedness, which challenges conventional perceptions of reality.

Central to Talbot's exploration is the enigmatic nature of holograms. Distinct from standard photographs, a hologram contains all the information of the whole within each fragment. Cut a hologram, and each piece still reflects the complete image, though at a reduced clarity. Analogously, Talbot posits, every part of the universe encapsulates a microcosmic reflection of the entire cosmos.

Talbot's groundbreaking insights are deeply rooted in the work of physicist David Bohm and neurophysiologist Karl Pribram. While Bohm's quantum theories hinted at a fundamentally holographic universe, interconnected at every conceivable point, Pribram proposed that our brain, too, operates holographically. Every fragment of our brain, he believed, played a part in our cognition, defying localized functioning.

Melding these perspectives, Talbot presents a staggering thesis: our reality might be a holographic projection, an interplay between our consciousness and deeper universal truths. Consequently, *The Holographic Universe* invites readers to transcend traditional beliefs about the tangible world, proposing a reality that's both a scientific marvel and a spiritual enigma.

Holonomic Brain Theory: Deciphering the Holographic Mind

Conceived by neuroscientist Karl Pribram and physicist David Bohm, the holonomic brain theory offers a radical perspective on the brain's functioning and information storage. It challenges the conventional belief of localized memory storage, proposing instead a brain that resonates with the principles of holography.

Pribram's theory is rooted in the fundamental attributes of holograms, where every fragment carries the essence of the entire image. Similarly, according to Pribram, memories aren't stored in isolated brain cells but are distributed across the brain. The brain, he postulated, processes visual cues in a manner akin to a Fourier transform holograph, interpreting information based on wave frequency patterns, not just localized regions.

The confluence of Pribram's neuroscience insights with Bohm's quantum physics speculations birthed a compelling narrative: that the universe might be a grand hologram. They proposed that quantum principles might govern cognitive processes, suggesting a mirroring of the non-localized, interconnected nature of quantum elements in brain functions.

This theory is profound in its implications. If the brain functions holonomically, it underscores a deeply interconnected cognitive architecture where every part is symbiotically linked to the whole. It also suggests an intimate connection between brain processes and the universe's fabric, insinuating a more intertwined reality than traditionally understood.

In essence, the holonomic brain theory, underpinned by holographic principles and quantum mechanics, presents an interconnected paradigm of brain function. A topic of ongoing research and debate, it offers a transformative perspective on understanding consciousness and reality's enigmatic nature.

Belief is a formidable architect of our reality. While it can empower and uplift, it can also constrain and confine. We must dare to question, seek, and understand to break free from the shackles of limiting beliefs and fears. Only then can we truly embrace the infinite possibilities that lie beyond.

Navigating the Labyrinth of Belief

Imagine for a moment that you are a fragment of the infinite divine energy of the Creator. Entering this realm, you embody human form and begin to explore the world you've manifested, a kaleidoscope of energy, vibration, and frequencies. As a sentient being, you engage with this realm in awe, allowing yourself to be enchanted and absorbing experiences that subtly shape your subconscious. Over time, these collected experiences solidify into core beliefs, guiding your voyage through life.

A primal emotion, fear, undeniably sits at the center of many of these beliefs. Anchored by our evolutionary fight-or-flight instinct, these fears gradually construct barriers and constraints around our existence. Ideally, our journey should be free from these impediments, a seamless path leading toward our most authentic selves. Yet, the scripts we unconsciously pen for ourselves erect walls that often hinder our progress.

Consider our collective response to the death of a loved one. Societal norms dictate a response of grief, sorrow, and longing. Anyone choosing to celebrate the life lived rather than mourn the life lost might be viewed as deviating from the acceptable path. Though deep-seated, such conventions exemplify the myriad walls we encounter.

True progress demands a reckoning with these barriers as we

meander through life. To break free from them, we must not merely find ways around; climbing over or sneaking beneath only offers fleeting relief. Instead, we must confront the foundational beliefs that erected these walls, striving to rewrite the scripts that hold us captive, for it's in our response to these walls that the keys to dismantling them lie.

Your inherent greatness has always been with you, undimmed by time or circumstance. The only thing obscuring its brilliance are the layers of self-imposed limitations. Everything you yearn for, every dream and aspiration, lies within reach, unbounded by societal or self-inflicted constraints. Understand that you are both the architect and the inhabitant of your reality. These walls of beliefs, though formidable, are of your own making. The walls crumble by shedding these weighty shackles, revealing a horizon teeming with boundless possibilities and the harmony of an existence aligned with the Creator's vision.

Questioning our Beliefs

At the heart of introspection and personal growth lies the imperative to question our beliefs. This process of challenging our convictions acts as a catalyst for intellectual and spiritual awakening. It enables us to strip away the layers of long-held assumptions, allowing us to delve into the core of our being and the essence of the world around us. We embark on a journey of profound self-discovery and understanding by confronting these deep-seated beliefs.

Throughout history, the influential role of belief in shaping human behavior has been acutely recognized by those in power. Rulers and influential figures have often crafted and disseminated dogmatic ideologies, typically steeped in fear, to maintain control. These fear-based dogmas act as psychological fortresses, offering their adherents an illusion of safety and certainty. Consequently, those who dare to challenge these entrenched beliefs often face persecution or alienation, as their critical perspectives threaten the status quo and possess the disruptive potential to instigate societal change.

This tendency to cling to the familiar, to beliefs ingrained in us from a young age, underscores the human fear of the unknown.

Minds enslaved by fear and unchallenged dogmas find false comfort within the confines of their self-imposed boundaries, perceiving these limitations not as barriers but as shields against life's uncertainties. Such minds are blind to the possibilities that exist beyond their mental prisons.

The endeavor to question and transcend these limitations is more than a mere intellectual pursuit; it is a profound journey toward emancipation. Breaking free from the shackles of unexamined beliefs is a transformative process, liberating our intellect and spirit. It invites us to venture into new realms of thought and existence, paving the way for fully realizing our potential. Engaging in this journey of liberation means stepping into a broader, more vivid reality, embracing the richness of a life unbound by unfounded fears and unquestioned dogmas.

In our quest for intellectual and spiritual freedom, the act of questioning our beliefs emerges as a vital step toward enlightenment. This introspective challenge propels us to uncover deeper truths that shape our existence, urging us to reassess the dogmas that have long dictated our lives. Such reevaluation reveals how these beliefs influence our behavior and, often, serve as tools for those in power to maintain control through fear-based ideologies.

As we pry open the doors of our mental enclosures, we realize that our journey doesn't end with liberation from these constraints. It leads us into the intricate web of belief systems that define our shared human experience. Here, religion and philosophy, two of the most fundamental structures of human thought, beckon us to delve deeper.

Religion, with its rich tapestry of traditions and rituals, offers a framework for many to find meaning and purpose. In the sacred spaces of temples, churches, mosques, and synagogues, individuals gather not just to worship but to connect with a community and a higher power. These belief systems, developed over millennia, shape the daily lives and worldviews of billions, providing answers to life's profound mysteries and moral guidance.

The transition from questioning personal beliefs to exploring the broader realms of religion and philosophy is a natural progression in our search for understanding. It prompts us to examine the collective beliefs that have shaped human civilizations and to reflect on how these resonate with our newfound perspectives. In this exploration, we engage with the vast spectrum of faith and thought that has sought to explain our place in the universe, enriching our journey of liberation with a deeper appreciation for the diverse ways humanity has sought to understand the cosmic dance of existence.

Religion and Philosophy: Navigating Belief Systems in our World

In the intricate tapestry of human existence, religion stands as a dominant thread, interwoven into the fabric of daily life. It offers systems of faith and worship, often connected to a higher power or a pantheon of deities, that guide millions in their everyday lives. These religious systems provide moral blueprints, imbuing life with a sense of purpose and striving to unravel the profound enigmas of existence. Across the globe, in diverse places of worship, such as temples, churches, mosques, and synagogues, people gather not only to seek spiritual guidance and solace but also to forge a sense of community. In these sacred spaces, individuals find a connection with a force that transcends human understanding, and these deeply rooted beliefs significantly shape their daily rituals, behaviors, and perceptions of their place in the cosmos.

Philosophy, the venerable companion of religion, invites individuals to engage in critical thinking, reflection, and the pursuit of wisdom. It provides a framework for understanding the world and our place within it, questioning the nature of reality, existence, and the complexities of human thought and behavior. Philosophers throughout history have explored the same profound questions addressed by religion, yet often through a lens of rational inquiry and logical reasoning. Where religion often relies on faith and divine revelation, philosophy leans on argument, debate, and a relentless quest for truth.

Together, religion and philosophy form a dynamic duo in the realm of human thought and culture. They address the fundamental questions of human existence: Why are we here? What is the purpose of life? How should we live? While religion often offers answers rooted in tradition and spiritual insight, philosophy challenges individuals to find their own answers through reasoning and personal reflection.

This intersection of religion and philosophy is evident in the various belief systems that dot the landscape of human culture. From the ancient philosophies of the East, such as Buddhism and Hinduism, which blend religious rituals and philosophical inquiry, to the Abrahamic faiths of Judaism, Christianity, and Islam, which each have rich philosophical traditions, these systems offer diverse paths to understanding life's greatest mysteries.

The relationship between religion and philosophy continues to evolve in the modern world. As societies become more secular, the influence of organized religion may wane, but the fundamental human need to understand our existence persists. Philosophy, with its emphasis on critical thinking and self-reflection, plays a crucial role in helping individuals navigate a world where traditional religious beliefs are increasingly questioned.

The journey through the realms of religion and philosophy is not merely an academic pursuit; it is a deeply personal journey that shapes one's identity, values, and worldview. As we explore these belief systems, we are challenged to consider our own beliefs, to question, to learn, and ultimately, to grow. This exploration is not just about finding answers but about understanding the questions themselves and appreciating the rich diversity of human thought and experience.

Religion and philosophy, as navigators of belief systems in our world, offer unique and complementary pathways to understanding life's most profound questions. They invite us to explore, question, and reflect, providing a rich tapestry of ideas and beliefs that help us understand our world and place within it.

Diving into Philosophical Tenets:

- **Solipsism:** Is a philosophy positing that only one's mind is certain to exist. Extreme solipsists argue that nothing beyond their consciousness exists, making the external world and other consciousnesses mere conjecture. Solipsism shakes the foundations of objective reality. It proposes that only our personal experiences and perceptions are verifiable truths, prompting questions about the nature of existence and our ability to truly understand anything beyond our immediate consciousness.

- **Determinism:** Is a philosophy asserting that all events, including human decisions, are preordained by external causes, implying that free will is illusory. Determinism ignites debates on morality. If our actions are predetermined, can we genuinely be held accountable for them? The ramifications of this belief ripple through areas from theology to law.
- **Fatalism:** This is the belief that all events are pre-set and thus inevitable, suggesting an inability on humans' part to alter the future. Fatalism emphasizes human powerlessness while echoing deterministic sentiments. It suggests that while events have causes, any attempt to change them is in vain.

Diverse Philosophical Alternatives:

- **Free Will:** The conviction that individuals possess the autonomy to make choices uninfluenced by prior causes. This contrasts starkly with determinism, suggesting an active human hand in charting life's course.
- **Indeterminism:** A counter to determinism, proposing that not all events have predetermined causes; some events could transpire spontaneously without prior causation.
- **Compatibilism (or Soft Determinism):** A synthesis suggesting determinism and free will aren't mutually exclusive. It posits individuals act based on their desires and motivations, even if these motivations have prior determinants.
- **Nihilism:** A perspective asserting life's inherent lack of meaning or value, leading to a rejection of moral constructs, religious principles, and value systems.
- **Absurdism:** Born from Albert Camus's thoughts, this philosophy acknowledges a chaotic, purposeless universe. Yet, it underscores the human drive to seek meaning, even in the face of inevitable failure.

These diverse philosophical ideologies and religious systems present myriad interpretations about existence, individual agency, and life's significance. Each offers its distinctive perspective on our roles and relationships within the vast universe.

Understanding diverse philosophical alternatives, like Free Will, Indeterminism, Compatibilism, Nihilism, and Absurdism, offers several benefits:

- **Broadens Perspective**: Exploring these philosophies expands one's understanding of different worldviews. It opens up a broader perspective on how various thinkers have interpreted fundamental aspects of human existence, such as choice, destiny, and purpose.
- **Encourages Critical Thinking**: Engaging with these diverse ideologies prompts critical reflection on one's beliefs and values. It challenges readers to consider and question the underpinnings of their assumptions about life, freedom, and morality.
- **Enhances Decision-Making**: Understanding these philosophical concepts can influence how one makes decisions. For instance, recognizing the debate between free will and determinism might lead to more thoughtful consideration of choices and the factors influencing them.
- **Fosters Tolerance and Empathy**: Learning about different philosophical viewpoints can foster greater tolerance for diverse opinions and beliefs. It can enhance empathy by appreciating why people may hold certain views about life and existence.
- **Provides Comfort or Challenge**: For some, these philosophies might offer comfort. For example, the idea of free will can be empowering, while for others, the concept of absurdism might resonate more deeply, providing a framework to navigate life's unpredictability.
- **Intellectual Engagement**: These ideas engage the intellect and stimulate mental exploration. They push the boundaries of conventional thinking and allow for a more profound engagement with life's big questions.
- **Navigating Life's Challenges**: Philosophies like compatibilism or absurdism provide frameworks to navigate

life's challenges. They offer ways to reconcile seemingly contradictory aspects of human experience, such as free will and determinism, or the search for meaning in a seemingly purposeless universe.

- **Influences Personal Growth**: Understanding and grappling with these philosophical concepts can be a part of personal growth. It encourages introspection and can lead to a deeper understanding of oneself and one's place in the world.

Exploring diverse philosophical alternatives enriches the reader's understanding of the human condition, challenges preconceived notions, and equips them with intellectual tools to navigate and interpret life's complexities.

Chapter 8 | The Power of Perception and Creation

"Reality is created by the mind; we can change our reality by changing our mind." – Plato

Our thoughts are potent entities, springing forth from the intricacies of our minds and shaping our very perception of reality. We process the world through our senses, creating a tapestry of experience that constitutes our existence. Without these senses and perceptions, our presence in this material world would be an enigma, rendering us intangible.

The realm of classical mechanics, with its Law of Conservation of Mass, would challenge the assertion that "Mind Creates Matter." It posits that mass neither emerges nor vanishes; it simply transforms. Picture a box of rocks: whether intact or shattered, their collective weight remains unaltered.

Yet, the arcane world of quantum mechanics introduces a riveting concept: matter assumes form only in the presence of an observer. If this premise holds, then it implies our beliefs, if fueled with enough fervor and conviction, have the potential to give birth to reality. It beckons us to question our existence: who or what perceives us, allowing us to exist? It's a philosophical conundrum akin to the age-old riddle: which came first, the chicken or the egg?

To shape your reality, there's a need for energy. Visualization is the first step, succeeded by belief. The collective consciousness, when synchronized in belief, amplifies this energy. Yet, it's essential to be wary, as emotions like envy or jealousy from this collective can siphon off the required energy, thwarting manifestations. Hence, it's prudent to shield one's aspirations unless one is certain of the collective's unadulterated intentions.

Envision life as a game where the very fabric of reality bends to our beliefs. In this game, you're both the creator and the participant, orchestrating a grand narrative only to revel in its unfolding.

Quantum physics is teeming with counterintuitive phenomena,

pushing the boundaries of our understanding and challenging our perceptions of reality. Heisenberg's uncertainty principle is central to this domain, a fundamental concept that encapsulates the inherent limitations in our ability to precisely measure specific pairs of complementary properties of a quantum system, such as position and momentum.

The Observer Effect and Quantum Mysteries

The observer effect, a related but distinct idea, delves deeper into the peculiarities of quantum mechanics. At its core, the observer effect highlights the perturbation of a system simply by the act of observation. This is not merely a byproduct of imprecise or intrusive measuring tools but a profound statement about the nature of reality at the quantum level.

Take the seemingly straightforward task of measuring the pressure in an automobile tire. Placing a gauge on the tire's valve releases some of the air inside, inherently altering the pressure we aim to measure. Similarly, observing non-luminous objects demands light to strike the object, prompting it to reflect that light and thus allowing us to see it. The process of observation, in these instances, is not passive; it intrinsically changes the state of the system.

Nowhere is this phenomenon more evident and puzzling than in the double-slit experiment. When particles such as electrons or photons are shot toward a barrier with two slits, and when not directly observed, they exhibit an interference pattern on a screen behind the barrier, indicative of wave-like behavior. However, the act of observing which slit the particle goes through collapses this wave-like behavior, and the interference pattern disappears, with particles behaving as if they are mere particles. This transformative nature of observation in the quantum world hints at a deep connection between consciousness and the fabric of reality.

The implications of these quantum phenomena suggest that our observation is not a mere passive process. Instead, it is deeply entwined with the behavior and nature of quantum systems. The observer effect and Heisenberg's uncertainty principle serve as a profound reminder of the intricate dance between observation and reality, challenging our conventional understanding and urging us to embrace the enigmatic beauty of the quantum realm.

The observer effect and quantum mysteries illustrate that our act of observing can fundamentally alter the state of what we observe, suggesting a deep entanglement between consciousness and the physical world. This principle, highlighted in the realm of quantum mechanics, poses intriguing questions about the nature of reality and our role within it.

Transitioning from the microscopic interactions of quantum particles to the macroscopic scope of human existence, we find that this notion of observation influencing reality extends beyond the confines of quantum physics. The profound secret of our existence might lie in a simple yet overlooked truth: our inherent ability to shape and be shaped by our surroundings.

Throughout history, humans, like all life forms, have reacted to their environment, often unaware of the reciprocal influence they exert. This interaction is not limited to the physical or observable; it extends to the very essence of creation and existence. Just as the observer effect shows that our observation can alter a particle's behavior, our collective reality is continuously shaped by our perceptions, beliefs, and actions.

Nature, in its pursuit of balance, echoes this concept. Our societal structures, cultures, and beliefs program us from birth, guiding us to interact with the world in specific ways. These interactions are not merely passive experiences but active engagements that can either harmonize with or disrupt the natural balance.

As we acknowledge the power of observation in quantum mechanics, we must also recognize our collective power in shaping our world. The knowledge of creation, thus, may not be concealed in unknown mysteries but in realizing the impact of our conscious and unconscious contributions to the tapestry of reality.

The Concealed Knowledge of Creation

Could the profound secret be a simple acknowledgment of what we've concealed from ourselves? Over eons, humans have been programmed to react to their environments, failing to recognize the reciprocal influence they exert. From microorganisms to majestic beasts, every life form exhibits this reactive trait. And yet, humanity, for all its intelligence, often overlooks its inherent power to shape collective realities. This notion, albeit faintly, resonates in esoteric teachings and certain religious scriptures.

Nature thrives on equilibrium, ensuring balance in every facet. From birth, societal programming orients us toward a pre-established script. We're conditioned to navigate the world through our senses, forming emotional bonds with experiences. But, at times, this very mechanism propels us towards imbalance, prompting attempts to control or obliterate these experiences, sometimes wreaking havoc on the environment.

While free will grants agency, it often confines us to mere reactions. However, awakening instigates a metamorphosis in our understanding, revealing the dormant power within. The notion of shaping one's reality is often rebuffed and deemed as overreaching. Yet, if nature crafts our experiences and we respond, then by the same token, we too can mold our reality, compelling nature to reciprocate.

However, such expansive thinking faces resistance from the collective, reminiscent of the crab-barrel mentality. Fear, an age-old tool, is wielded to divert attention from this latent power. Those who dare challenge the established script face ridicule and ostracism, ostensibly to curb the spread of their enlightenment.

Yet, beneath layers of societal constructs and self-imposed limitations lies a monumental force. We unearth this dormant potential by shedding these barriers and critically examining our beliefs.

Embrace this revelation: You are the Creator, and within you resides unparalleled power.

The Interplay of Perception and Belief

Perceptions serve as the choreographers in the intricate dance of existence, directing our actions and reactions. These perceptions are not mere passive reflections of the external world; our beliefs actively mold them. Every belief we hold acts as a lens, coloring and shaping how we interpret the world around us.

Imagine your beliefs as the foundation of a grand edifice, with perceptions being the rooms, hallways, and windows. These structures determine how you navigate and interact with your environment. A belief, whether formed through personal experience, cultural conditioning, or learned knowledge, acts as the blueprint, dictating the architecture of perception.

For instance, if one holds a belief rooted in scarcity, they may perceive opportunities as limited, seeing the world through a lens of competition and deprivation. Conversely, someone with a belief anchored in abundance might view the same circumstances as rife with possibilities and potential collaborations.

The potency of beliefs goes even further when we recognize that they're not always rooted in conscious acknowledgment. Subconscious beliefs, often established in our formative years, can silently drive our perceptions without explicit awareness. These undercurrents can sometimes contradict our conscious beliefs, leading to internal conflicts and incongruences in our actions.

Furthermore, as beliefs shape perceptions, they create a feedback loop. The way we perceive situations and events reinforces our beliefs. If one believes in their inherent lack of talent and perceives every challenge as evidence of this belief, they unwittingly strengthen this self-limiting conviction. Breaking free from such a cycle demands introspection and a willingness to challenge and revise deeply held beliefs.

Given the profound influence of beliefs on perceptions, it becomes imperative to cultivate self-awareness. Periodic self-reflection and mindfulness practices can help identify and recalibrate beliefs that no longer serve our growth. By intentionally choosing our beliefs, we wield the power to craft perceptions that align with our aspirations and values.

In essence, while perceptions sculpt the reality we experience, our beliefs chisel out these perceptions. Recognizing this interrelation equips us with the tools to not just passively experience life but to actively shape it in alignment with our most authentic selves.

Understanding the interplay of perception and belief illuminates how our internal states (thoughts, beliefs, and attitudes) shape our reality. This notion extends beyond the psychological into the physical realm, particularly when considering reality's vibratory nature and sound's power. Just as beliefs mold our perceptions and, by extension, our life experiences, the energy we emit through our thoughts and emotions can influence the very fabric of reality.

Imagine this: The universe, at its core, is a tapestry of vibrations. Each thought, feeling, and belief we hold resonates like a note in an immense cosmic symphony. This perspective aligns with the understanding that every particle, every piece of matter, and, indeed, the entire universe, is in a state of constant vibration, emitting frequencies that interact with each other.

Our beliefs and perceptions, therefore, are not just mental constructs but vibrational patterns that can align with or discord with the universe's symphony. When we tune our internal vibrational energy (our thoughts, emotions, and beliefs) to a particular frequency, we are essentially tuning into a specific aspect of the physical reality, much like tuning a radio to a desired station.

Thus, the power of our beliefs to shape our perceptions is mirrored in the power of our vibrational energy to influence our reality. Just as we can choose and reshape our beliefs to align with our true selves and aspirations, we can also consciously adjust our vibrational frequency to attract or manifest different aspects of the physical world. The principle that we attract what we vibrate toward suggests that by embodying the energy of what we desire, be it through belief, emotion, or intention, we can draw those experiences and entities into our lives.

While the interplay of perception and belief reveals the profound impact of our internal states on our personal experiences, the concept of the vibratory nature of reality expands this influence to a universal scale, where the power of sound, frequency, and vibration plays a pivotal role in shaping the world around us.

The Law of Perception: Shaping Reality Through Our Lens

The Law of Perception posits that our reality is not just a direct reflection of the external world but is significantly shaped by our interpretations, beliefs, and experiences. Simply put, we don't just see the world as it is; we see it as we are. Our perceptions filter and color the raw data of the external environment, giving rise to our unique version of reality.

Every individual has a unique set of experiences, beliefs, cultural backgrounds, and personal biases. These elements form a perceptual lens through which we interpret the world around us. Two individuals, for instance, can witness the same event and come away with vastly different interpretations and feelings about it, all due to their perceptual filters. This underscores the idea that reality is subjective and is co-created by our minds.

Understanding the Law of Perception is crucial because it affects every aspect of our lives, from relationships to decision-making. Recognizing that our perceptions might not always represent objective reality can help us keep an open mind, empathize with others, and be more adaptable in our interactions. Furthermore, by becoming aware of and challenging our biases and preconceived notions, we can work toward a more transparent, more objective understanding of the world, reducing misunderstandings and conflicts. The Law of Perception reminds us of our minds' powerful role in constructing our realities, emphasizing the importance of self-awareness and understanding in navigating the world.

The Vibratory Nature of Reality and the Power of Sound

The concept of "The Vibratory Nature of Reality and the Power of Sound" dives into the foundational belief that vibration is at the core of our universe. Every entity, from atoms to galaxies, is in a state of constant vibrational motion, emitting unique frequencies of energy. This concept likens the universe to a grand symphony, where every object and element emits its own distinct note or frequency.

By tuning into these frequencies, much like adjusting a radio to find a specific station, it's believed that we can attract the energy of specific matter or outcomes to ourselves. This idea suggests that deeply believing and feeling as if a desired goal or object is already in our possession can draw that reality closer to us.

The power of sound is a profound manifestation of vibrational energy. Words, chants, mantras, and prayers are more than just linguistic constructs; they are creators of vibrations that can influence and reshape matter. This is evident in phenomena like sand forming intricate patterns on a vibrating speaker or the unique sound frequencies produced by running fingers around a wine glass rim or striking a singing bowl.

Music and sound frequencies, especially those tuned to 432 Hz or 528 Hz, are believed to have healing properties. This isn't just a mystical claim but has been explored scientifically. For instance, pioneers like Royal Rife and Dr. Anthony Holland used Oscillating Pulsed Electric Fields to explore resonant frequencies, and experiments have demonstrated the potential to use sound for feats like levitating objects.

Moreover, the concept of 'junk DNA' in our genetic makeup, which is not fully understood, raises questions about whether these DNA segments could be influenced or programmed through vibration. Experiments connecting an oscilloscope to a 432 Hz frequency, a universally harmonious sound, suggest profound possibilities, aligning with Nikola Tesla's theories on controlling resonant systems.

In medical science, therapies like Pulse Electromagnetic Field (PEMF) therapy use energy waves for treatment, highlighting the interplay between energy, frequency, and wellness. However, perception plays a crucial role in how we interact with and understand vibrational energy. The diversity in human perception, as illustrated by various internet debates, shows that our beliefs, experiences, and imagination significantly shape our perceptions.

In essence, this perspective views the universe as an immense, resonating entity. By understanding and utilizing these vibrations, we have the potential not just to interact with but also to shape our reality. This symphony of the universe, where energy, vibration, and frequency intermingle, suggests that everything in existence, from cosmic entities to the smallest particles, is perpetually in motion, resonating with unique frequencies that we can learn to harmonize with and influence.

The Potency of Sound

Galileo once posited that our senses construct our reality. Just as an architect visualizes a structure before laying its foundation, our perceptions craft our external world. Every atom, every molecule in our universe, hums at its unique resonant frequency. Pioneers like Royal Rife and Anthony Holland, MD, delved deep into this field; Holland explored Oscillating Pulsed Electric Fields, illustrating the universe's intricate dance of energies.

Examples abound showcasing the potency of resonant frequencies, from levitating objects using sound waves to the mysteries of junk DNA. Could it be that this so-called junk DNA is not redundant but potentially programmable?

Using an oscilloscope, John Stuart Reid's experiments showed a universal connection to 432 Hz. Meanwhile, the visionary Nikola Tesla claimed, "If we can control that resonate system electronically, we can directly control the entire mental system of mankind."

Contemporary practices like Pulse Electromagnetic Field (PEMF) therapy channel these principles, directing potent energy waves into individuals to facilitate healing and well-being.

Our collective perception of reality is not infallible; it can sometimes present illusions, such as the internet's famous white or gold dress conundrum or deceptive impressions of footprints in the sand. Our unique experiences, beliefs, and cognitive frameworks tailor our interpretations. Our beliefs especially sculpt our perceptions. After all, how can one truly perceive what one has never dared to imagine?

To echo the words of Andrew Carnegie: "Any idea that is held in the mind, that is emphasized, that is either feared or revered, will begin at once to clothe itself in the most convenient and appropriate form available."

In essence, our universe is a grand orchestration of energies, vibrations, and frequencies. By understanding and harnessing these, we can perceive our reality more clearly and shape it in unimaginable ways.

Perception and Power: The Double-edged Sword

In our approach to life's challenges, we often fall into a pattern of immediate reaction. This behavior is deeply ingrained in us: when we face a problem, our instinct is to confront it head-on. However, the essence of a problem lies not in its inherent nature but in how we perceive it. Our minds play a crucial role here, quickly labeling and characterizing any problematic situation. This rapid identification and reaction inadvertently empower the problem, giving it a life and presence in our world that it might not inherently possess.

This phenomenon is a classic case of perception shaping reality. Typically, we respond, react to, or resist problems, which only serves to amplify their impact on our lives. Yet, if we shift our perspective, the problem often loses its daunting aspect. Instead of avoiding or fighting it, we can confront it head-on, dissect its core, and understand it for what it really is: a matter of perspective, often clashing with our deep-rooted beliefs. As I discussed in the initial chapters of my book, drawing upon Robert Scheinfeld's insights, overcoming emotional attachments is key to unlocking the lessons embedded in these challenges. By fully engaging with the situation, staying present, and embracing the learning opportunity, we take back the power we've unintentionally given to the problem. In reality, each obstacle is a lesson in disguise, holding the seeds of its own resolution within it.

When we view problems through an abundance mindset, their nature fundamentally changes. Based on the belief in the plentifulness of resources and opportunities, this mindset transforms problems from barriers into opportunities for growth and learning. Adopting this perspective, we approach challenges with optimism and creativity, viewing them not as roadblocks but as avenues for gaining new insights, fostering innovation, and driving improvement. This proactive stance encourages resilience and a focus on potential positive outcomes, leading us to innovative solutions, effective collaboration, and a willingness to learn and adapt, ultimately enhancing our well-being.

In stark contrast, a scarcity mindset leads us to perceive problems as insurmountable obstacles. Rooted in the belief that resources and opportunities are limited, this perspective often incites fear, stress, and a defensive approach. Here, problem-solving becomes reactive, focusing on averting immediate losses rather than seeking long-term growth. This approach, colored by pessimism and a fixed mindset, results in competitive and rigid solutions that fail to recognize the potential for personal and collective development inherent in challenges. Understanding these dynamics is crucial in redefining our approach to problems and transforming them into opportunities for profound growth and learning.

Embracing True Power: Beyond Fear

Now, let's delve into fear's profound impact on our lives, subtly eroding our inherent power. Our conscious mind, the aspect of ourselves we're fully aware of and present to the world, crafts our personal narrative and identity. However, beneath this visible layer lies the subconscious mind, a vast repository of past programming, emotions, and deeply ingrained beliefs. From an early age, this part of our psyche absorbs and internalizes experiences, shaping the scripts that underpin our conscious thoughts and actions. It's through these subconscious beliefs that we often unknowingly inject our perceptions with fears and expectations, thereby dictating much of our life experience.

The core of our struggle often lies in a deep-seated desire for control, fueled by the fear that things might not go as planned. We set up defenses and create obstacles to avoid unwanted experiences, paradoxically missing out on crucial life lessons. This fear-based approach to control and a lack of trust in the flow of life is precisely where we inadvertently relinquish our true power.

To reclaim this power, a shift in mindset is essential. However potent it may seem, fear is ultimately grounded in a narrative shaped by societal conditioning and personal experiences. Overcoming this narrative requires learning from our experiences and embracing gratitude for the lessons they provide. This process involves redirecting our energy from fear and control to trust in the natural course of life. It's in the realization and acceptance of our innate magnificence and potential that true empowerment begins.

This empowerment is not just about overcoming fear; it's about rewriting the subconscious scripts that have long dictated our responses to life's challenges. It involves consciously reprograming our mindset, replacing fear and doubt with trust, openness, and a deep understanding of our inherent worth. By doing so, we don't just cope with life's vicissitudes; we thrive, using each experience as an opportunity to grow and expand our horizons. In embracing this new way of being, we unlock a level of power and potential within ourselves that transcends our old fears and limitations, allowing us to become the fullest expression of who we truly are.

Now that we have explored the transformative journey of overcoming fear and reclaiming our inherent power by shifting our mindset. We learned that our conscious mind crafts our identity, while our subconscious, laden with deep-seated beliefs and emotions, subtly orchestrates much of our life experience. This journey of empowerment is not just about conquering fear; it's about reprogramming the subconscious narratives that dictate our responses to life's challenges. By replacing fear and doubt with trust and a deep recognition of our worth, we evolve beyond mere survival, thriving in the face of life's complexities and embracing our fullest potential.

In the next chapter, our focus turns to the ego, the facet of ourselves that we knowingly display to the world. Serving as the custodian of our individuality, the ego significantly influences how we perceive and engage with our experiences. It acts as the prism through which we view our reality, shaping our personal stories and giving them meaning. This exploration of the ego is as crucial as our earlier discussions on transcending fear and reprogramming our subconscious. In the realm of collective consciousness, which can be likened to an immense theater, the ego assumes roles beyond mere performance. It is not only a participant in the narrative but also the narrator, converting our inner beliefs and convictions into lived experiences. As we delve into the essence of the ego, we will examine how it molds our perception of reality and identify ways to disentangle its influences, paving the path toward a more genuine and empowering existence.

Chapter 9 | The Ego and Beyond: Sculpting Our Reality and Unraveling Attachments

"Attachment is the root of suffering." – Buddha

At the heart of our self-conception lies the ego, a persona, an identity we consciously present to the world. As a guardian of our individuality, the ego interprets and interacts with the myriad experiences that life offers. Without it, our understanding of reality would blur, and our narratives would lack form and purpose. While it brings our beliefs and convictions to life, the ego also becomes our compass, helping us find our way through societal expectations and cultural norms.

Imagine our collective consciousness as a sprawling theater. Within this expansive stage, every entity dances to the rhythm of a universal consciousness. Our personal beliefs shape every step and move, our internal scripts. Here, the ego is not just an actor but also a storyteller, translating these scripts into tangible experiences.

From the moment of our birth, our mental canvas remains untouched, pure from societal imprints. As we journey through life, every interaction acts like a brushstroke, molding our perceptions and, in turn, shaping our ego. This evolved perception, akin to an artwork, stands protected and is often reluctant to change. Daring to question or redefine it might mean confronting our most deeply rooted fears and insecurities.

However, the ego isn't the antagonist of our life's story. It is both a seductive and protective force, guiding and sometimes misleading us. While it is born from our beliefs and experiences, confronting it is less about conflict and more about understanding. To know oneself fully requires introspection into the ego's intricate labyrinth.

Rather than suppressing the ego, our goal should be to find harmony with it. It's a creation molded by our experiences and can be reshaped by revisiting and recalibrating our core beliefs. Mastering oneself involves recognizing the ego's role in shaping our reality, ensuring it facilitates rather than dominates our experiences.

Emotions, intangible and complex, serve as the lifeblood of our existence. They anchor us, giving depth and color to our reality. These emotions, emerging from our intricate web of beliefs, often make us latch onto experiences: be it treasured memories, intense feelings, or the shimmering beacon of hope. This clinging, while adding depth to our life's narrative, can also overshadow our true essence.

Life presents itself as a mosaic of experiences, each a lesson nudging us toward a broader understanding of reality. Exploring the universe's fabric, contemporary science proposes that everything might be reducible to binary codes. Such patterns then culminate into the diverse forms we witness around us. Pioneering experiments, like the double-slit, suggest that reality morphs through our observations, which are deeply influenced by our beliefs. Emotional attachments to these experiences amplify their impact, making them resonate longer.

Attachment: The Illusory Bond

The concept of attachment as an illusory bond delves deeply into the notion of liberation, particularly in the context of spiritual and personal growth. Liberation, as understood in this context, is a multifaceted and deeply personal state, varying in its meaning from one individual to another. For some, it represents an escape from the everyday confines of life, while for others, it signifies a higher state of consciousness. But to truly understand liberation, one must first comprehend the concepts of 'grasping' and 'non-grasping.'

Grasping is a fundamental aspect of human nature. It refers to our tendency to cling to various aspects of our lives: material possessions, memories, beliefs, relationships, and even our own perceptions of reality. This tendency stems from a deep-rooted desire for stability and predictability in an inherently transient and ever-changing world. As humans, we naturally gravitate towards what is familiar and comforting, often as a defense mechanism against the unpredictable nature of life. However, this grasping leads to attachments that can cause suffering as we struggle to maintain a sense of permanence in an impermanent world.

On the other hand, non-grasping is presented as a philosophical and practical antidote to the problems posed by attachment. It is not merely a concept but a way of living that encourages us to experience the flow of life without trying to control, redirect, or contain it. Non-grasping teaches us to be fully present in each moment, to appreciate life in all its raw and unfiltered beauty, without the burden of undue attachment.

The transformative power of non-grasping can be broken down into several key insights:

- **The Ephemeral Nature of Life:** Understanding and accepting the transitory nature of life and everything in it can lead to a profound sense of liberation. By releasing our tight grip on our experiences and relationships, we are able to appreciate them more fully for the temporary wonders they are.
- **Authentic Freedom:** Letting go of attachments allows us to view the world from a new perspective. It opens up an inner space of freedom beyond mere physical or external freedom, leading to a sense of expansiveness within.
- **Inner Tranquility:** By moving away from the habit of grasping, we can find a sense of peace and calm that remains steady, even amidst life's inevitable storms.
- **Genuine Relationships:** Approaching relationships without a desire to control or possess leads to more authentic and meaningful connections characterized by mutual respect and affection.
- **The Beauty of the Present:** Embracing non-grasping allows us to live fully in the present, free from the shadows of the past and anxieties about the future.

Adopting a non-grasping approach can be challenging in our modern world, where possession and achievement are often seen as synonymous. It requires a conscious effort to unlearn long-held habits and to reconnect with our true selves. This journey involves practices like mindfulness, meditation, and intentional detachment, guiding us toward a deeper understanding of our being.

U.G. Krishnamurti's View on Attachment

U.G. Krishnamurti, known as the "anti-guru," was a 20th-century philosopher whose views on spirituality and enlightenment were unconventional and often controversial. His teachings starkly contrasted with traditional religious and spiritual doctrines, primarily focusing on the pointlessness of many spiritual pursuits.

A central theme in Krishnamurti's teachings is the concept of impermanence. While this idea has roots in ancient philosophies like Buddhism, Krishnamurti gave it a unique twist in his discourse. He emphasized that everything in existence, including our emotions, physical bodies, and the world around us, is constantly changing. Nothing is static.

Krishnamurti believed that much of human suffering arises from our quest for permanence in an impermanent world. We often cling to beliefs, relationships, material possessions, and personal identities, hoping they will offer lasting security and purpose. However, the transient nature of life means that these anchors are bound to change or disappear, leading to disappointment and pain.

Krishnamurti's teachings become particularly intriguing when he discusses the pursuit of impermanence. Unlike most spiritual teachings that encourage accepting impermanence to alleviate suffering, Krishnamurti suggested that the act of seeking itself, whether for permanence or acceptance of impermanence, is the root of sorrow. He argued that this seeking implies a sense of lack or the need to fill a void, keeping individuals in a state of continuous dissatisfaction.

To escape this cycle of suffering, Krishnamurti advocated for a radical halt to all forms of seeking. He proposed a state of "not-knowing" or "unbecoming," where individuals let go of all attachments, including desires, beliefs, and ingrained notions. In this state, people are not constrained by past, societal expectations, or future aspirations. Instead, they live in the present moment, free from mental constraints and the burden of expectations.

Krishnamurti's approach challenges many established spiritual and philosophical ideologies. He invites individuals to face their deepest fears and desires, suggesting that true freedom doesn't come from finding answers but from stopping the search altogether. His perspective on attachment and impermanence is unique and thought-provoking, proposing that real freedom isn't about achieving enlightenment or personal growth but letting go of pursuing these goals and living in the present, unburdened by past or future concerns.

Building on U.G. Krishnamurti's profound teachings about the nature of attachment and the pursuit of impermanence, we are led to contemplate the broader implications of these insights on our everyday lives. Krishnamurti's philosophy, which challenges us to relinquish our constant search for answers and live in a state of "not knowing," aligns closely with the concept of embracing life's inherent fluidity. Just as he advocates for a release from the constraints of our desires, beliefs, and societal expectations, we find a similar thread in understanding the ephemeral nature of existence.

"The Key to Letting Go" reflects this philosophy by likening life to a continuously flowing river, where each moment is precious due to its fleeting nature. This metaphor beautifully encapsulates the idea that recognizing and appreciating the transitory nature of life can lead to a deeper enjoyment of the present. It's a call to embrace Krishnamurti's impermanence, to live fully in each moment without being weighed down by the past or anxious about the future.

Furthermore, this concept underscores the importance of detachment. Just as holding onto water in a river is impossible, so is clinging to past moments or memories. This understanding echoes Krishnamurti's teachings about the futility of seeking permanence in an impermanent world. Letting go becomes an art form, a necessary skill for personal growth and openness to new experiences and insights.

Emotional Attachments: Tipping the Scales

While experiencing life, it's natural to form emotional bonds and attachments to moments, people, and outcomes. However, problems arise when these attachments, driven by intense emotions, tether us to specific outcomes or past experiences. Think of these attachments as weights, tipping the balance of our internal scale.

For instance, when we hold onto feelings of resentment or anger or create elaborate expectations around love, we add weight to one side of our balance. Having intense emotions or harboring certain expectations creates 'emotional karma.'

As we navigate life's ever-changing landscape, the transient nature of our experiences serves as a reminder to cherish the present and be adaptable, ready to evolve with time's flow. Embracing the impermanence of life, as both Krishnamurti and the philosophy of letting go suggest, offers a path to a future replete with possibilities and unburdened by unnecessary attachments. This approach not only aligns with Krishnamurti's teachings but also offers a practical application of his philosophy in our daily lives, guiding us toward a more liberated and fulfilling existence.

The Key to Letting Go

The key to letting go as a concept is enriched by awareness that resonates deeply with the fluid and ever-changing nature of life, mirroring the continuous flow of a river. In this analogy, each moment is likened to a droplet in a vast river, valued not for its permanence but for its fleeting presence. Heightened awareness brings into focus the ephemeral quality of life, fostering a deeper appreciation for the present. This conscious recognition allows us to relish every aspect of our current experiences. Moreover, this awareness highlights the vital lesson of detachment. When we fully comprehend the transient nature of our past experiences and memories, we understand that clinging to them can impede our growth. Thus, Awareness becomes a key tool in mastering the art of letting go, helping us see the need to release our grip on the past to make room for new experiences and insights.

However, understanding life's fluidity also underscores the importance of detachment. Holding onto past experiences or memories too tightly, akin to trying to grasp the water in a river, is futile and counterproductive. Letting go is not about erasing or dismissing our past; it's about loosening the hold these experiences have on us, enabling us to move forward unburdened. This act of releasing creates space for new experiences, fostering growth and evolution.

Moreover, life's transient nature serves as a constant reminder of the value of the present moment. While it's natural to reflect on the past or plan for the future, becoming too fixated on these can detract from fully experiencing the present. Embracing impermanence, the understanding that nothing in life is static, keeps us adaptable and open to change. By letting go of attachments to the past and outdated perceptions, we can flow with the life changes, just as a river smoothly navigates the twists and turns of its course.

The essence of letting go is found in embracing life's perpetual state of change, valuing the present moment, and understanding the importance of detaching from past experiences. By recognizing and accepting life's impermanent nature, we free ourselves from the burdens of the past and open ourselves to a future brimming with possibilities, growth, and fulfillment. This philosophy encourages us to fully engage in each moment, prepared to evolve alongside the natural progression of time. This path leads us toward a journey of personal freedom and potential, where we can live our lives to the fullest, unencumbered by what has been and open to what can be.

The Elegance of Letting Go

At the core of our existence is a sequence of ephemeral moments. Every second we live, unfolds an experience, teaches a lesson, and then gracefully fades away. Embracing and subsequently releasing these moments is the very pulse of life. Yet, our emotional entanglements often trap us, causing us to cling to these fleeting instances. This tethering halts our progress, shackling us to the past and obstructing the path to new experiences. To truly evolve, we must internalize the transitory nature of life and permit ourselves to ride its ebb and flow without getting entangled.

Delving deeper into this philosophy, Taoism, an ancient Chinese tradition, offers profound wisdom. Central to Taoist thought is the concept of 'Wu Wei,' which, at its surface, translates to "non-doing" or "non-action." However, this doesn't advocate passivity. Instead, it emphasizes action that harmonizes with the universe's inherent rhythm, actions that feel effortless because they align with life's natural ebb and flow.

In his seminal work, the Tao Te Ching, Lao Tzu introduces the idea of the Tao or the Way. This isn't just a path but the fundamental essence that weaves through every facet of existence. To act in harmony with the Tao is to embody Wu Wei. When we achieve this alignment, our actions become a spontaneous dance in tandem with the universe's cadence. It's not an absence of intent but a profound synchronization with the cosmic rhythm.

For a more precise illustration, envision water, a central motif in Taoist allegories. Water flows unhurriedly, never contending, yet it's potent and always finds its way. In this fluidity, Taoism sees a guidepost. By embracing the Wu Wei principle, we learn to navigate life with agility, determining when to surge forward and when to pause, ensuring our actions resonate with nature's inherent balance.

Wu Wei, in its purest essence, is not a call to detach from the world but an invitation to engage with it in an authentic manner. It encourages us to let go of our obsessive need for control and trust in the universe's innate wisdom. By allowing life to unfold in its natural rhythm, we embrace its beautiful unpredictability, moving gracefully amidst life's turbulence. This approach requires us to recognize the forces of karma, be mindful of the emotional imbalances we create, and consciously strive to realign ourselves. Achieving this balance leads not only to inner peace but also to a harmonious connection with the universe's delicate dance.

In a similar vein, understanding love requires moving beyond superficial interpretations and letting go of attachment. Love, often misconstrued and sought to fill voids or seek validation, is deeply ingrained in our lives. It's fundamental to our relationships, yet its true nature extends far beyond conventional understanding. This journey of understanding love teaches us that its essence isn't found externally but exists inherently within us, as we are the embodiment of love. Over time, societal norms have obscured our perception of love, presenting it as a mere shadow of its true self. Genuine love emanates from a place of deep compassion and altruism, transcending societal constraints. As philosopher Alan Watts put it, love involves surrender but also a deep understanding of what it is not. It surpasses formal commitments and physical expressions, radiating unconditionally from our being. This realization echoes the principles of Wu Wei, where the act of letting go and embracing the natural flow leads to a deeper, more authentic engagement with life and love.

Understanding Love: Beyond the Superficial and Letting Go of Attachment

Love is a profound yet often misunderstood concept. It is a sentiment deeply ingrained in every aspect of our lives, from daily conversations to literature and art. Despite its ubiquitous presence, comprehending the true essence of love remains a nuanced and complex task. Love forms the foundation of our relationships, but its true nature goes far beyond superficial understandings.

Fundamentally, love is frequently sought to fill a void or seek validation, leading us to depend on others for emotional fulfillment or attributes we feel are missing within ourselves. However, this journey towards understanding love brings us to a critical realization: the essence of love is not something to be found externally. It exists inherently within each of us. We are, in essence, the very embodiment of love.

Over time, societal norms and expectations have clouded our perception of love, often portraying it as a diluted version of its true self. Genuine love transcends these societal limitations, originating from a place of deep compassion, altruism, and unconditional emotions. It's an innate quality that cannot be pursued or contained; it simply radiates from our being.

Philosopher Alan Watts described love as "an act of surrender to another person." Yet, this surrender also involves understanding what love is not. It goes beyond formal commitments like marriage or physical acts like sex. These might be expressions of love but do not fully represent its essence. In its purest form, love is unconditional and cannot be adequately captured in words.

Love's most profound manifestations often occur in moments of adversity, sacrifice, and compassion. Acts of bravery, comforting someone in distress, or empathy towards those in need exemplify love's true nature. Similarly, our relationships with animals often reflect unconditional love, where silent, unspoken bonds signify a pure and unadulterated form of love.

The journey towards true love begins with self-acceptance and self-love. Embracing our true selves can radiate authentic love outward, leading to more meaningful and enriching interactions. In this context, the Hebrew word "Caleb," meaning "dog," symbolizes loyalty and unwavering affection, mirroring the unconditional nature of love seen in our animal companions.

Ironically, the pursuit of love can be paradoxical. The more we seek it, the more elusive it seems. Often, in moments of quiet introspection, away from the external world's distractions, we discover the joy associated with love has always resided within us. Letting go of the attachment to love as something to be attained externally allows us to understand its true form: a spontaneous and boundless essence that flows from within. Love is not about possession or dependence; it's a free-flowing energy transcending superficial attachments. By embracing this understanding, we realize that we have always embodied love in its most authentic form.

Liberation: The Ethereal State of Non-Grasping

Every soul aspiring for spiritual and personal growth invariably encounters the enlightening concept of 'liberation.' But this term, multifaceted in its essence, raises a poignant question: What does liberation genuinely represent? To some, it evokes the idea of breaking free from the confinements of day-to-day existence. To others, it epitomizes an ascended state of consciousness. Yet, to truly comprehend this emancipated state, we must first acquaint ourselves with the contrasting realms of 'grasping' and its more evolved counterpart, 'non-grasping.'

Human nature, in its very essence, is tethered to the act of grasping. This extends from tangible material possessions to intangible memories, deeply ingrained beliefs, cherished relationships, and even our perceptions of reality. The root of such attachment lies in an instinctive yearning for constancy in a world marked by fleetingness. Even as the cosmos whirls in perpetual change, humans innately cling to what's known and comforting, often out of apprehension for the unforeseeable shifts of life. Such attachments, born out of grasping, frequently lead us into the throes of suffering.

The philosophy of 'non-grasping' emerges as a beacon of wisdom against this backdrop of attachment. More than just a concept, non-grasping is a way of life. It teaches us to let the river of existence flow unhindered without our incessant attempts to redirect, control, or cage it. Far from advocating a passive stance towards life, non-grasping urges us to immerse ourselves in the moment, savoring life's raw beauty without the trappings of undue attachment.

Adopting the non-grasping approach can seem daunting in our contemporary world, where possession is often misconstrued as achievement. Yet, like all profound arts, it mandates dedication, perseverance, and time. The path is strewn with lessons of unlearning age-old habits and reacquainting oneself with the essence of true being. Mindful practices, meditative reflections, and intentional detachment can guide us on this transformative odyssey. As we journey forth, it becomes lucid that genuine liberation isn't in accumulating more but in the graceful art of non-grasping.

To encapsulate, *Liberation: The Art of Non-Grasping* is more than a philosophy; it's a call to delve deeper into the realms of true freedom. It underscores the realization that genuine liberation isn't an external accolade but a profound internal awakening. By striking a harmonious balance between active engagement and unbridled attachment, we sail through life's vast oceans with grace, poise, and unparalleled wisdom.

Liberation: The Quest for Inner Freedom

Liberation, in its most profound sense, is freeing the self from the chains of external circumstances and internal afflictions. Across philosophies, spiritual teachings, and even psychological frameworks, the idea of liberation encapsulates a journey from bondage to freedom, from ignorance to enlightenment, and the temporal to the eternal.

Let's delve deeper into this concept using an illustrative analogy. Imagine a house with sturdy walls and transparent windows. Outside, the weather changes constantly: sometimes there's brilliant sunshine, other times torrential rain, and occasionally, the ferocity of a storm. But inside the house, it's tranquil, unaffected by the vagaries of the external environment. The house doesn't prevent the outside events from occurring; instead, it provides shelter, ensuring that these externalities do not disturb the peace within.

We can liken liberation to this inner sanctuary. It suggests that while we cannot always control or change what happens around us, we can determine how it affects our internal state. Pursuing liberation teaches us not to let external circumstances infiltrate our inner peace. It's about recognizing that while we are in the world, we do not have to be of it in such a way that every external fluctuation throws us into chaos.

The mention of becoming ambivalent and indifferent to experiences might raise eyebrows, especially in cultures emphasizing passionate engagement with life. However, these terms take on a deeper, more nuanced meaning in the context of liberation. Being ambivalent or indifferent doesn't denote a lack of care or apathy toward life. Instead, it suggests a detached involvement, a capacity to engage with experiences without being ensnared by them. It means appreciating life's joys without becoming overly attached and facing adversities without being unduly dismayed.

Expanding and transitioning from a discussion about letting go of attachments in spiritual traditions to the concept of Karma-Yoga in the Bhagavad Gita's third chapter, we delve deeper into understanding how our actions shape our spiritual journey.

In many spiritual traditions, attachments are seen as the anchors that hold us down, preventing us from realizing our true, liberated nature. They are the strings that tug at our hearts, drawing us into the tumultuous seas of desires, fears, and illusions. To let go of these attachments is not to renounce life's pleasures or to adopt an ascetic existence. Instead, it's about experiencing life fully without the clinging, the fear of loss, and the burdensome weight of possession.

Achieving such liberation is undeniably challenging, especially in a world that constantly pulls our attention outward. Yet, with introspection, mindfulness, and a genuine understanding of the impermanent nature of life, we can cultivate inner resilience. Over time, this resilience helps us remain centered and balanced, allowing external events to unfold without letting them disturb our internal equilibrium. In this state, we truly experience freedom, realizing that liberation is not an external destination but an inner journey of letting go.

This concept of liberation ties intricately into the teachings of the Bhagavad Gita, particularly in its third chapter, which elucidates the essence of Karma-Yoga. The Bhagavad Gita, an eternal testament to life and its many facets, expounds on the interplay of actions (karma) and their consequences.

The third chapter highlights that the physical world is in perpetual motion, making absolute inaction an illusion. Every entity, whether knowingly or unknowingly, partakes in myriad actions. The nature of these actions, however, is pivotal in shaping our spiritual journey. Actions driven by worldly desires entangle us in the ceaseless cycle of birth and rebirth, binding us to the very attachments we seek to transcend.

In contrast, actions performed in the spirit of Karma-Yoga, detached from personal gains and outcomes, have the power to liberate. Such actions, when executed without attachment to their results, can illuminate our path toward spiritual enlightenment. Herein lies the quintessence of Karma-Yoga as portrayed in the Bhagavad Gita's third chapter: the realization that true liberation and enlightenment are achieved not by renouncing action but by embracing it in its purest form, free from the shackles of personal desire and attachment. This harmonizes with the earlier notion of letting go, suggesting that true freedom and spiritual enlightenment come from understanding and practicing the art of detached involvement in our actions.

The essence of Karma-Yoga, as portrayed in the Bhagavad Gita, teaches us about actions performed without attachment, which illuminates the path to enlightenment and liberation. This concept seamlessly transitions into understanding the universal principle of balance. Just as the Bhagavad Gita emphasizes the importance of detached action for maintaining spiritual equilibrium, the broader universe, too, operates on a principle of balance, which is integral to its very design.

In its infinite wisdom, nature meticulously ensures that a harmonious equilibrium is maintained, gracefully navigating between balance and imbalance in the grand ballet of existence. This rhythm, ancient and profound, underpins the universe's operations. Nature's tireless efforts to maintain harmony, juxtaposed with moments when abundance tips the scales, reflect a profound dichotomy. It's a paradox that is not accidental but emblematic of the universe's deeper principles.

At the center of this cosmic dance is evolution, a process that drives the universe forward, continually evolving and diversifying. Yet, there are times when evolution reaches a point of saturation, a moment where further growth or diversification becomes counterproductive. In these moments, nature enters a phase of introspection, leading to deconstruction or even atrophy. However, this is not an end but a transformation, a stage where consciousness, in its purest form, emerges as a pivotal force.

This consciousness, pristine and unadulterated, is like an artist before a blank canvas, full of potential and possibilities. As it gains self-awareness, it realizes its inherent power and begins to shape and diversify, initiating a new cycle of evolution. These transitions from simplicity to complexity are fundamental to the nature of existence.

In this vast cosmic landscape, the concept of time, so precious to human understanding, assumes a different dimension. Time becomes fluid, transcending the linear progression of past, present, and future. In this realm, events from the beginning, middle, and end of our perceived timeline converge into a singular, continuous now. Every transition we experience, from birth to rebirth, occurs simultaneously, offering a transformative revelation about the nature of existence and the simultaneous nature of our journey through it.

Chapter 10 | The Eternal Equilibrium: Navigating the Dance of Balance and Imbalance

"Life is a balance of holding on and letting go."
– Rumi

Balance is integral to the universe's design. In its infinite wisdom, nature meticulously ensures that a harmonious equilibrium is maintained. Nature gracefully moves between balance and imbalance in the grand ballet of existence. It's a rhythm as ancient as time itself, perpetual and profound.

There's an intriguing dichotomy at play here. On the one hand, nature tirelessly works to maintain harmony, but when abundance becomes unrestrained, the very equilibrium it seeks is disrupted. This paradox is not a mere cosmic accident; it's emblematic of the universe's underlying principles.

At the heart of this dance is evolution, a process that continuously propels the universe forward. But occasionally, evolution reaches a saturation point where further growth or diversification becomes counterproductive. In these moments, nature reverts to a phase of introspection, leading to deconstruction or even atrophy. However, this isn't a terminal state; it's a transformative one. It's in this state that Consciousness, in its most elementary form, takes center stage.

This Consciousness, pure and untainted, is much like an artist staring at a blank canvas, brimming with potential. As it gains self-awareness, it realizes its inherent potency and starts to shape and diversify, spawning a new cycle of evolution. Such transitions from simplicity to complexity are at the heart of existence.

Now, considering time, that ephemeral construct humans hold dear, we find it takes a different hue in this vast landscape. Time becomes fluid, with events from the beginning, middle, and end of our perception all coalescing into a singular *now*. Every moment, every transition we experience, from birth to rebirth, is happening concurrently. It's a revelation that reshapes our understanding of existence, underscoring the simultaneous nature of our journey.

Delving deeper, creation itself is an enigma. The inherent duality in existence, where opposites coexist, creates a dynamic tension vital for growth and experience. This oscillation between balance and imbalance, creation and recreation, isn't a mere happenstance; it's the universe's chosen path for growth and evolution. Such experiences, replete with contrasts, enrich our souls, providing depth and wisdom.

Yet, everything seeks a return to balance, for an endless state of chaos would lead to existential entropy. It's a journey that isn't about regression but evolution, armed with the lessons imbalance teaches.

Drawing parallels with enlightenment, it becomes evident that our existence isn't solely about seeking a state of perpetual balance. It's about recognizing and appreciating the ebb and flow intrinsic to life. Embracing this dance, our lives, marked by their highs and lows, serve as a testament to this universal rhythm. As we partake in this cosmic ballet, we don't just seek peace; we yearn for the profound wisdom that the journey between balance and imbalance offers. In this understanding lies our true purpose, anchoring us in unity, wonder, and an ever-evolving sense of being.

The Universal Law of Balance

At its core, Karma reflects the universe's method of maintaining balance and harmony. It can be viewed as the spiritual counterpart to Newton's third law. Similar to how physical actions generate corresponding reactions, our thoughts, actions, and emotions initiate a series of ripples that echo across the cosmos. This principle implies that every decision, sentiment, and intention we hold releases a wave of energy, ultimately returning to us in some form or another. This cycle of actions and reactions, governed by the principle of Karma, underscores the interconnectedness of our actions and their broader impact on the universe.

Karma: The Cosmic Balance Sheet

Karma, in its essence, represents the universe's method of sustaining balance and harmony. It can be seen as a spiritual analogy to Newton's third law. Just as physical actions elicit corresponding reactions, so do our thoughts, actions, and emotions set into motion a series of ripples that reverberate throughout the cosmos. This principle suggests that every decision, sentiment, and intention sends out a wave of energy, which eventually circles back to us in some form.

This idea of Karma transcends mere cause and effect; it's a cosmic balance sheet where our deeds, good or bad, are meticulously accounted for. It's an ongoing process of checks and balances, ensuring that the universe remains in a state of equilibrium. Just as a pebble tossed into a pond creates an expanding circle of ripples, our actions and emotions have far-reaching consequences, propagating through the fabric of the universe.

In this view, the universe operates not just as a system of physical laws but as a moral and spiritual entity. Our actions, thoughts, and emotions are not isolated events but integral components of a vast, interconnected system. The law of Karma underscores the interconnectedness of all things and the inherent responsibility that comes with this realization. By understanding and aligning ourselves with this universal law of balance, we not only contribute to the equilibrium of the cosmos but also navigate our lives with a deeper sense of awareness and purpose. This realization brings us to a profound understanding of our place in the universe, not as mere observers or passive participants but as active contributors to the cosmic dance of balance and harmony.

Nature's Perfection and Humanity's Place Within It

Nature, in its infinite complexity, is a testament to perfection. Yet, as humans, we often perceive ourselves as flawed fragments of this grand design. Intelligence is a relative concept, and while humans are lauded for their cognitive prowess, every living organism possesses its own brand of intelligence, perfectly attuned to its needs. Humans are particularly unique in their tendencies to consume, possess, and sometimes disrupt their natural surroundings. Much like a virus or weed operates in its ecosystem, humans, too, seem designed to engage with their environment in specific, impactful ways. However, to say humans offer nothing to their surroundings is an oversimplification. Every entity, including humanity, plays its role in the intricate dance of ecological balance.

Nature operates on principles of balance and cyclicality. It responds to imbalances by introducing counterbalances; when one element becomes too dominant, nature may introduce challenges to restore equilibrium. Yet, just as with any evolutionary process, there comes a point where further evolution appears stagnant or counterproductive. When this peak is reached, nature might engage in processes of renewal or transformation, which might appear as self-destruction on the surface.

This cyclical phenomenon traces back to the foundational essence of existence: consciousness. Everything emerges from consciousness, becoming aware of its potential, evolving into tangible forms, growing, peaking, and eventually returning to its primal state.

As we understand it, the concept of time is a mere construct. Every phase of this cycle (creation, flourishing, dissolution, and rebirth) unfolds simultaneously in the grander scale of existence. As conscious beings, we are perpetually living our beginnings, endings, and renewals, all in the present moment.

Harmony in Nature and Nature's Paradox: Humanity's Role in Balancing the Ecosystem

Nature, in all its magnificence, thrives on balance. Every organism, every ecosystem, and every natural process plays a part in maintaining this delicate equilibrium. In their unique position, humans serve as disruptors and balancers. They are the imperfection that challenges nature, pushing it to recalibrate, adapt, and evolve. This seeming contradiction, that humanity's flaws lead to nature's perfection, is a complex idea that requires exploration.

Unlike many species, humans don't always integrate seamlessly into their environment. Their impact often resembles that of a virus or an invasive species, consuming resources and altering habitats at an alarming rate. This tendency was poignantly described by the character Agent Smith in the movie *The Matrix*. He observed that humans tend to overwhelm their environment while most mammals develop a symbiotic relationship with their surroundings. They consume, expand, and move on, leaving behind changed landscapes.

While comparing humans to viruses is stark, it offers a mirror to reflect upon our actions and intrinsic nature. Like a virus, humans have the capacity to spread and consume, but they also have the ability for reflection, change, and restoration. It's this duality, the potential for both destruction and healing, that sets humanity apart.

However, with this duality comes responsibility. The same tendencies that allow humans to dominate also grant them the power to restore and rebalance. Humankind stands at a crossroads: on one path lies unchecked consumption and inevitable self-destruction, and on the other, a journey towards harmony, both internally and with the world around them.

Until humans achieve inner balance and recognize their interconnectedness with nature, they will continue to grapple with their role in the natural order. But with introspection and action, there's hope. The potential for humans to act as stewards rather than mere consumers is immense. By finding harmony within, humanity can forge a new, sustainable relationship with the world, shifting from being seen as a 'disease' to becoming the cure nature seeks.

In conclusion, humanity's relationship with nature is intricate and multifaceted. While their actions may sometimes resemble those of a virus, the potential for change, growth, and restoration is deeply embedded in the human spirit. As they journey towards inner balance, they hope to find harmony with the natural world, ensuring a brighter, more sustainable future for all.

The Quintessence of Karma-Yoga in the Bhagavad Gita's Third Chapter

The Bhagavad Gita stands as an eternal testament to life and its many facets. The third chapter of the Bhagavad Gita highlights the delicate interplay of deeds and their repercussions within its sacred verses.

The physical world is in perpetual motion, rendering absolute inaction an illusion. Every entity, be it knowingly or unknowingly, partakes in myriad actions. Yet, the very nature of these actions shapes our spiritual voyage. Some actions, driven by worldly desires, bind us to the ceaseless cycle of birth and rebirth. Others, however, can illuminate our path toward spiritual enlightenment.

The Bhagavad Gita presents profound teachings that resonate

through time, and its relevance is evident when we consider the concept of trusting the natural process in our lives. Central to the Gita's teachings is the idea that the intent behind our actions is more influential than the actions themselves. Actions driven by self-centered desires or egocentric motives entangle us within the intricate web of karma, binding us to the material realm. In contrast, actions become liberating forces when performed as tributes to the Divine, free from personal desires or attachments.

This shift in perspective is epitomized by Karma-yoga, a concept highlighted in the Gita's third chapter. Karma-yoga involves performing worldly duties with a heart deeply rooted in divine love, harmoniously blending duty and devotion. By channeling our actions toward divine pleasure and service, we transcend the bounds of individual karma. Engaging in selfless service, we remain unaffected by the outcomes of our actions, be they positive or negative. Instead, we align ourselves with a purpose far grander than our individual selves, thus disentangling from the confining grip of karma. This path paves our way to the ultimate liberation, an aspiration that resonates with the essence of trusting the natural process of life.

Transitioning to the philosophy of embracing the flow of life, we find a similar thread of wisdom. In the intricate dance of existence, filled with twists, turns, and unexpected rhythms, the notion of trusting the natural process emerges as a guiding light. This belief anchors us in the understanding that life, with all its mysteries, unfolds in alignment with a greater wisdom or cosmic design. It encourages us to navigate life's course with faith, patience, and open-hearted acceptance, much like how Karma-yoga advises us to approach our actions.

Observing nature, we witness a harmonious symphony that gracefully ebbs and flows. Trees, for instance, embrace the changing seasons without resistance. They exist in the moment, embodying patience and the understanding of perfect timing. This natural rhythm of nature is a gentle reminder that we, too, will thrive in our own time. Just as Karma-yoga teaches us to perform our duties with devotion and without attachment to outcomes, trusting the natural process of life invites us to embrace life's unfolding journey with a similar spirit of acceptance and grace.

Both these philosophies, whether derived from the ancient wisdom of the Bhagavad Gita or from observing the natural world, guide us towards a similar realization: the path to liberation and harmony lies in aligning ourselves with a higher purpose and embracing life's journey with faith and open-heartedness. In this alignment, we find a deeper connection to the world around us and an inner peace that transcends the fluctuations of our daily experiences.

Trusting the Natural Process: Embracing the Flow of Life

We often encounter twists, turns, and unexpected rhythms in the intricate dance of existence. Amidst these complexities, the philosophy of trusting the natural process stands as a beacon of hope. This belief anchors us in the conviction that life, with all its myriad mysteries, unfolds in alignment with a greater wisdom or cosmic design. It encourages us to navigate its course with faith, patience, and open-hearted acceptance.

Looking to nature, we find a guide in its harmonious symphony that ebbs and flows gracefully. Trees, for instance, embrace the changing seasons, neither lamenting the fall of leaves nor hurrying the bloom of flowers. They simply exist in the moment, exemplifying patience and the magic of perfect timing. This observation gently nudges us to realize that, like nature, we too will flourish when our time is right.

Often, life's unpredictability can stir a storm of emotions within us. However, a significant portion of our anguish stems from resisting what is currently happening. By embracing the natural flow of life, we transition from battling the currents to floating effortlessly. This dance of surrender, where acceptance makes us light, guides us gracefully through life's waters.

Each moment in life is rich with lessons waiting to be discovered. When we trust that every event, whether delightful or daunting, serves a purpose, our perspective shifts. We transition from questioning our experiences to understanding and embracing them as stepping stones that refine and enrich our journey.

Life's tapestry is a blend of familiar patterns and mysteries that elude our grasp. Trusting the process means acknowledging this balance and meeting the unknown not with trepidation but with a spirit of adventure and wonder. This approach fosters resilience, transforming challenges into opportunities to display our inner strength. It reassures us that after every storm, there is a rainbow, and after each night, a new dawn awaits.

For many, this trust transcends the physical realm and touches the spiritual. It connects us to a higher wisdom, offering solace and suggesting that a benevolent force ensures our journey aligns with a purpose larger than our immediate understanding.

True strength, paradoxically, lies in surrender. Releasing our grip and relinquishing control is not a sign of weakness but an emblem of true power. It signifies alignment with the rhythm of life, ensuring that our voyage remains harmonious and filled with grace.

Celebrating the journey is an integral part of trusting the process. Life's essence is not confined to grand milestones but is vividly present in everyday moments. To trust the process is to cherish each step, find delight in fleeting moments, and recognize their intrinsic value.

Undergoing the profound transformation that comes with embracing the philosophy of trusting the natural process shifts our perspective. We move from the shadows of doubt to the light of acceptance, finding serenity amidst the storm, understanding amidst the unknown, and a bond with the universe's ineffable rhythm. As we sail on this journey, we are reminded that we are not mere observers but active participants, painting our life's canvas with hues of experiences, insights, and perpetual growth.

PART THREE: The Destruction

Chapter 11 | The Real You

"Reality is an illusion, albeit a very persistent one." – Albert Einstein

Reality as we perceive it is a construct, a mosaic built upon individual and collective consciousness. Envision our existence as players on a vast game board. Although we each possess unique perspectives, we all play in the same realm, mistakenly thinking the game is reality. Emotions, sensations, and feelings, as we know them, were born from human conventions. These conventions are designed to give credence and depth to our experiences. But if humans have conceived these feelings, can they not be termed illusions? Understanding this can enable us to rebalance our energies and harmonize with nature.

Humans appear as nature's creation when we observe the world from a terrestrial perspective. Nature inherently seeks equilibrium. When it detects an imbalance, it acts to restore harmony. Humans, however, do not always align with nature's rhythm. Our survival instincts sometimes lead us to dominate nature rather than coexist. On a metaphysical plane, what if humans were meant to be nature's tool to rectify an overabundance of certain elements, like excessive trees or animals? Armed with cognitive abilities, humans have the potential to control and change nature's course.

Consider this analogy: An inventor identifies a need and builds a prototype device. Recognizing its potential, they then mass-produce it, refining and improving with each iteration. Similarly, humanity has evolved, adapting and growing into sophisticated beings, distinct from our primitive counterparts.

Central to our existence is the concept of free will.

The Power of Free Will

Possessing consciousness enables us to generate karma. Exercising free will can lead us away from our natural balanced state, inducing suffering unless we reconcile and release the karma. The stored energy of suppressed emotions finds a parallel in our physical form, causing ailments that resonate with the nature of the suppressed emotion.

Health, or the lack of it, is influenced by our beliefs. Diseases manifest in the body, often incubating first in the mind through sustained beliefs. The environments we immerse ourselves in also have the power to influence our mental and physical states. Collective emotional responses in environments like movie theaters or funerals underscore the influence of group dynamics on individual emotions.

Drawing inspiration from the film *The Invention of Lying*, there was a time when truth was the only language known to man. But, one lie, birthed from compassion, changed the course of human interactions. This anecdote highlights that our emotions, feelings, and even states of being, such as health or sickness, are societal constructs. Societal norms and expectations shape our understanding of them.

Being unwell isn't just about the manifestation of the disease; it's also about the perception of it. Our bodies are battlegrounds where microorganisms are constantly at war, ensuring our well-being. Similarly, our minds are arenas where thoughts clash and coalesce. The beliefs and thoughts we nurture directly shape our experiences. When we confine ourselves to societal constructs, like how an ailing person should behave, we inadvertently trap ourselves within those defined boundaries.

In essence, our perceptions, molded by collective consciousness, define our reality. But, by stepping back and examining these constructs, we can empower ourselves to transcend societal expectations and truly understand our essence.

The Black Plague, also known as the Black Death, was one of the most devastating pandemics in human history, killing an estimated 75-200 million people in Europe during the fourteenth century.

When the Black Plague hit Europe in the fourteenth century, it left an indelible mark on history. This deadly disease, caused by the bacterium Yersinia pestis, spread like wildfire and was extremely contagious. As it ravaged entire communities, people died in unprecedented numbers; it's estimated that up to 60 percent of Europe's population was wiped out.

Yet, not everyone succumbed to the disease. Even though

millions died, some seemed to be immune or resilient to the effects of the plague. Many factors could have contributed to this immunity, including genetic factors, previous exposure to other diseases, or sheer luck.

Some individuals, driven by compassion, altruism, or duty, risked their lives to care for the afflicted, fully aware of the danger. These caregivers included physicians, priests, family members, and groups like the Alexian Brothers, a Catholic religious order that cared for plague victims.

One explanation for their bravery might be rooted in their perception and beliefs. In times of crisis, people often turn to their deeply held beliefs and values to guide their actions. Some might have believed caring for the sick was their religious or moral duty. In contrast, others might have believed in the power of human connection and compassion in the face of overwhelming adversity.

The psychological theory of cognitive dissonance, introduced by Leon Festinger in 1957, suggests that individuals seek consistency when faced with information or situations that contradict their beliefs or perceptions. For instance, those caring for the sick might have minimized the perceived threat of the disease or believed that their protective measures would suffice.

The Black Plague and its impact on Europe provide a compelling lens to understand the power of belief and perception. Even in the face of a terrifying and seemingly unstoppable disease, human resilience, compassion, and the drive to find meaning and purpose in chaos came to the fore.

The Delicate Balance of Free Will in a Divine Framework

In exploring the delicate balance of free will within a divine framework, we encounter profound existential questions. The concept of an omnipotent deity overseeing life's chessboard presents a complex paradox. Each piece, from the humble pawn to the commanding queen, seems to have its moves preordained on this cosmic board. The pawn, though limited in mobility, possesses the potential to upend a queen, yet its nature confines it to specific moves. This deterministic orchestration raises the question: Does such a preordained design eclipse the possibility of genuine free will? True free will, it would seem, hinges on autonomy, a space where choices are sculpted not just by destined paths but by one's personal convictions and worldviews.

Destiny, often romanticized, is envisioned as a meticulously laid-out path for soul enrichment. However, the beauty of the human spirit lies in its defiance, in choosing pathways diverging from the ordained. Life, in its cunning, often reveals alternate routes when we stray, either nudging or catapulting us back on track. This defiance can birth internal turmoil as many journey down paths deviating from their core essence, yet destiny's siren call persists, awaiting acknowledgment.

This narrative intersects with the societal dynamics of our world. History shows civilizations oscillating between unity and division, influenced by perceptions of otherness. Such divisions create alliances and hierarchies, often dominated by factions whose power is rooted in personal ambitions. Fear, coupled with mechanisms of conformity, is used to maintain societal equilibrium, discouraging challenges to the established order. Media, religion, and education become tools to reinforce these boundaries, subtly guiding the populace's adherence. In response, individuals often turn to artificial respite (pharmaceuticals, therapy, or alternative liberations like psychedelics), only to find these avenues, too, are often constrained.

As power is acquired and jealously guarded, those at the helm employ tactics to maintain their omnipresence. A challenge to this order quickly brands one as a dissident, often leading to exclusion or more severe consequences. Society, in turn, drifts toward a herd mentality, celebrating mediocrity while suppressing curiosity and imagination. Entertainment forms like sports and music serve dual roles, providing escape while reinforcing societal bonds.

Transitioning to "Destiny's Dance: The Matrix of Free Will and Fate," we delve into the paradox of free will versus destiny. This paradox, which has intrigued philosophers and thinkers for centuries, explores the tension between destiny, suggesting our lives are preordained, and free will, proposing the power of independent choice. Destiny implies that our lives are part of a cosmic script, while free will champions personal agency and responsibility. This tension is vividly illustrated in "The Matrix," where Neo's journey reflects the struggle to reconcile these forces. His path, seemingly predestined, is also shaped by his decisions, posing the question: Can any action be truly free if everything is preordained?

The paradox of free will versus destiny is not merely theoretical; it profoundly impacts our daily lives, influencing our perception of reality, personal aspirations, morality, and ethics. It invites us to ponder the depths of human existence, challenging us to consider whether our lives are a prewritten narrative or a canvas painted with our choices. This profound question continues to captivate and inspire introspection and debate, weaving together the existential, societal, and philosophical threads that shape our understanding of life's intricate dance.

Destiny's Dance: The Matrix of Free Will and Fate

"Destiny's Dance: The Matrix of Free Will and Fate" delves deep into the profound questions about our place in the world and the essence of our choices, encapsulating the paradox between destiny, which implies a predetermined path, and free will, suggesting our power to shape our fate. This paradox, illustrated through Neo's journey in "The Matrix," challenges us to ponder if cosmic forces script our lives or if we have the autonomy to forge our own paths. The film artfully depicts this conflict, questioning the authenticity of freedom in a possibly predestined world.

This philosophical inquiry naturally leads us into the realm of herd mentality. This psychological phenomenon, where individual judgment is often sacrificed for group conformity, is influenced by various factors: the need for acceptance, the security in numbers, and the simplification of complex choices. Herd mentality can have merits, particularly in urgent situations requiring collective action. However, its more sinister aspects (leading to economic bubbles, harmful societal trends, and mass hysteria) cannot be ignored.

Combatting the adverse effects of herd mentality requires fostering introspection and self-awareness. By understanding these societal dynamics, individuals can make decisions that align with their true nature. Society is ever-changing, often shaped by group dynamics and power struggles. Dominant groups, driven by power consolidation, use fear to control and suppress dissent, with media, religion, and education playing pivotal roles in enforcing societal norms.

This social tapestry becomes even more intricate with manipulating and suppressing individuality. Challenging societal norms is not merely an act of defiance but is often seen as a moral transgression. Mavericks who question the established order risk ostracization, their dissent threatening the fragile societal balance. Even leisure activities like sports and music can reinforce herd mentality, offering temporary relief while perpetuating collective norms.

In this context, the free will versus destiny paradox takes on even greater significance, compelling us to reflect on the extent of our autonomy and the influence of societal and destined paths on our choices. Are we truly free in our decisions, or do unseen societal and cosmic forces shape them? This intricate interplay between individual agency and collective norms prompts a deeper exploration of human nature and the determinants of our destiny.

Adding a fascinating dimension to this exploration is the concept of a multiverse. Rooted in theoretical physics and science fiction, the multiverse theory proposes that each exercise of free will and every choice we make might open a new reality within an expansive multiverse. This theory posits multiple, perhaps infinite, universes parallel to our own, each representing a different reality with varied outcomes. Thus, each decision could be a branching point, potentially creating a new universe that follows the path of the alternative choice.

The implications are profound, suggesting that exercising free will might involve creating entire worlds of possibilities, transforming each choice from a singular event into a cosmic-scale phenomenon. This notion aligns with quantum mechanics, particularly the idea of quantum superposition, where all possible outcomes exist simultaneously until a choice is made, crystallizing a specific reality.

While the multiverse theory remains largely speculative and a subject of ongoing scientific debate, it provides an intriguing perspective on the implications of our choices. It suggests that our decisions could have far-reaching consequences, not just in our universe but in creating entire new universes of possibilities, adding a profound layer to the concept of free will.

Navigating the Labyrinth of Herd Mentality

Herd mentality, with its intricate psychological underpinnings, witnesses individuals forsaking personal judgment to meld with group norms. This behavioral spectrum is influenced by varied facets: the innate desire for acceptance, the solace found in numbers, the allure of simplifying convoluted choices, emotional synchrony in groups, and diminished personal responsibility in a collective.

There are contexts where herd mentality shines: emergencies, for instance, where collective action can be the lifeline. Yet, its shadow side cannot be ignored. It can catalyze economic bubbles, detrimental societal trends, and unfounded mass hysteria. A remedy? Cultivating introspection and self-awareness. Understanding these dynamics can empower individuals, equipping them to navigate societal pressures and make choices that resonate with their essence.

Societies, over millennia, have been arenas of dynamic flux, often shaped by perceived group differences. These perceptions solidify affiliations, carving out stark divisions. Every evolving society witnesses a dominant group's rise, their motives often gravitating toward power consolidation. They craft mechanisms ensuring their supremacy with their ascension, often sidelining dissent. Fear becomes their tool, deployed to ensure a seamless societal fabric.

In this societal dance, the media, religious institutions, and educational systems aren't mere spectators; they are often puppeteers. Their evolved roles serve not just to inform or enlighten but to delineate societal frameworks. Any deviation is quickly labeled, pushing individuals towards 'acceptable' solutions. The few who tread alternative paths, like psychedelics, find their pursuit of freedom riddled with societal bindings.

This elaborate societal mosaic is interwoven with manipulation threads. Here, challenging norms isn't a mere act of defiance; it's a moral deviation. True mavericks, those challenging this matrix, face ostracization lest their ideas disrupt the fragile equilibrium.

Entertainment avenues, from sports to music, offer more than leisure. They provide transient relief while immersing individuals in collective euphoria, strengthening herd mentality's roots. Within this framework, the genuine tragedy isn't the imposed restrictions but the voluntary, often passionate, acceptance of these confines. The chains that bind aren't just crafted by society but are often embraced by individuals in a poignant quest for belonging.

Understanding the Herd Mentality and Its Effects on Individuality

The concept of herd mentality centers on the human instinct to seek safety in numbers. This instinct fosters a sense of belonging and comfort, as individuals often find it easier to adopt the thoughts and behaviors of the majority. This inclination towards conformity leads people to align with the larger group, motivated by a desire for acceptance and an aversion to conflict. However, this phenomenon can be swayed or dominated by a few influential figures who may dictate specific moral standards or rules, expecting adherence from others. Their goal is often to instill a sense of order and predictability, molding societal behaviors to fit their vision of acceptability.

While there are advantages to having a structured community with shared values, this can also have negative implications. Excessive enforcement of the majority's beliefs can suppress individual creativity and expression, leading to a cultural environment where maintaining the status quo takes precedence over innovation and diverse perspectives. Consequently, those who diverge from these norms may feel constrained or marginalized, potentially resulting in frustration and rebellious tendencies as they strive to assert their unique identities and ideas.

In essence, while herd mentality can offer a framework of belonging and order, it's crucial to balance this with the encouragement of individuality and the appreciation of different viewpoints. Such a balance can foster a society that is both cohesive and dynamically diverse.

The Dance between Enlightenment and the Material World

The pursuit of enlightenment is a pivotal theme across various spiritual and philosophical traditions, often depicted as an elevated state of awareness, free from the confines of the material world. This pursuit involves transcending earthly attachments and realizing a higher, universal truth. Yet, this transcendence raises a question: does enlightenment necessitate a complete disengagement from the material world?

Suppose enlightenment leads to a profound detachment from worldly matters. In that case, it might hinder meaningful engagement with the tangible aspects of life, potentially isolating the enlightened from the common human experience. However, a deeper understanding of enlightenment might not lie in escaping the material world but in achieving a harmonious existence within it. This approach implies recognizing the fleeting nature of the material world while still valuing and participating in its unique experiences.

This concept aligns with the path of the bodhisattva in Buddhism, where enlightened beings choose to delay their liberation to help others attain enlightenment. This path exemplifies a selfless dedication to aiding others, harmonizing the enlightenment experience with the responsibilities of the material world.

A parallel can be drawn with Western mythology, specifically with Charon, the ferryman in Greek mythology who transports souls across the River Styx. Charon symbolizes a bridge between two realms, the living and the dead. Although different from the bodhisattva, the metaphor of an intermediary remains pertinent. Charon maintains a balance, serving as a connector between the tangible and the ethereal.

In conclusion, enlightenment might not be about escaping the material world but rather understanding and embracing its role in the broader spectrum of existence. True enlightenment could involve recognizing the divine in all things, acknowledging the interconnectedness of life, and engaging in the world with compassion and purpose. Like the bodhisattva and Charon, the enlightened being may serve as a conduit between the material and spiritual realms, illuminating the path for others in both worlds.

Butterfly (farfalle) Transformation

The Butterfly (Farfalle) Transformation poetically illustrates the transformative journey of self-discovery, deeply aligned with the essence of "The Real You." This metamorphosis, echoing the transition from a ground-bound caterpillar to a majestic butterfly, symbolizes the human awakening from the confines of ingrained beliefs to an expansive consciousness. It's a journey marked by significant changes in perception, beliefs, and actions, emblematic of the process of realizing one's true self, free from societal expectations and internalized beliefs.

The Cocoon of Conformity

On this path, the cocoon of conformity symbolizes the societal, cultural, and familial influences that shape our beliefs and actions. Analogous to the caterpillar's limitations, we are often confined within conventional thinking, hindering the realization of our full potential. This stage represents our detachment from "The Real You," the genuine self that lies hidden under layers of societal conditioning.

Moments of Introspection and Awakening

The transformative chrysalis stage reflects the pivotal moments in our lives when introspection or significant experiences challenge our long-standing beliefs. Triggered by life-altering events, exposure to diverse cultures, or a quest for truth, these moments initiate our journey toward discovering "The Real You."

Emerging as the Authentic Self

Breaking free from the cocoon, much like challenging conventional thinking, involves a journey fraught with obstacles. This process, often accompanied by cognitive dissonance and isolation, is vital for developing resilience and moving closer to "The Real You." This emergence marks a rebirth into an authentic existence, aligning decisions and beliefs with our true selves.

Thriving in Authenticity and Continuous Growth

As the butterfly thrives post-emergence, so do we, experiencing a profound shift in our worldview upon awakening. We cultivate a deeper appreciation for life, a zeal for exploring new ideas, and a passion for sharing our insights. This phase signifies the embodiment of "The Real You," free from societal constraints and driven by a purpose that echoes with our authentic self.

The journey of self-discovery and transformation is an ongoing process. Like butterflies experiencing multiple life cycles, we undergo numerous introspections and growth phases, each drawing us nearer to a more profound understanding of ourselves and the universe. It's a relentless pursuit of understanding and embracing "The Real You."

Awakening at the Crossroads: The Choice Between Comfort and Spiritual Evolution

We stand at the crossroads of choices in every moment of our lives. These decisions, big or small, can lead to a journey of ease or challenge, happiness or discontent. But among all our choices, the most profound is the decision to either remain in the comfort of our existing beliefs or to challenge them and awaken to a deeper understanding.

For many, there's a familiar solace in the predictable. We often cling to societal norms, beliefs, and patterns that provide a semblance of security. These conformist attitudes and the desire to maintain the status quo are not merely habits but also protective mechanisms. They shield us from the discomfort of confronting the unknown or questioning the foundations of our understanding.

Yet, true spiritual evolution demands that we stretch beyond the familiar. It requires us to entertain the idea that our current understanding is limited, that the knowledge we hold dear might only be a fraction of the vast universe of truths. For instance, consider the provocative thought that central religious teachings could potentially guide followers toward a misunderstood concept of divinity. What if these teachings obscured the true nature of the divine spark within us all, making us believe in our limited human potential rather than recognizing our inherent divinity?

Visualize a scenario where you start to tap into this dormant power within. Throughout your life, there have been subtle nudges, moments of clarity, urging you to awaken from the slumber of routine beliefs. Those who ignore these nudges continue in their life's cycle, often feeling a sense of unfulfillment, thinking that perhaps this mundane existence is all there is to life. But a profound transformation begins for those who heed the call and awaken. They start to grasp that their destiny has always been in their hands. Their self-imposed limitations have been the only barrier to accessing this latent power and potential.

With this newfound awareness, one embarks on a transformative journey akin to the metamorphosis of a caterpillar into a butterfly. Life's myriad experiences evolve from mere happenings to profound lessons that sculpt and refine the essence of our souls. This shift in perception moves us away from the shallow waters of ego-driven decisions and societal approval. Instead, it anchors our choices in a deeper, more meaningful understanding of the universal dualities that govern existence.

In this enlightened state, every aspect of life is viewed through a lens of wonder and appreciation. We begin to perceive the intricate tapestry of existence, woven with threads of contrasting experiences - joy and sorrow, success and failure, love and loss. These dualities no longer appear as conflicting forces but as harmonious counterparts, each playing a vital role in the grand design of life.

The beauty of life's dance becomes ever more apparent, revealing the interplay of light and shadow, strength and vulnerability, growth and decay. This perspective allows us to embrace life's complexities with grace and gratitude, understanding that every experience, whether perceived as positive or negative, contributes to the enrichment of our being.

In this state of heightened awareness, the once-ordinary moments are imbued with a sense of wonder and significance. The simple act of watching a sunset, the laughter of a child, or the quiet introspection during a solitary walk become profound experiences, enriching the soul in unexpected ways. Life is no longer a series of unrelated events but a cohesive journey of growth and discovery.

This metamorphosis brings about a profound inner peace as one aligns with the rhythm of the universe. With this alignment, choices and actions are guided not by fleeting desires or external pressures but by a deep, resonant truth that echoes the wisdom of the ages. This is a journey of awakening, where every step and choice leads one closer to their true essence and the boundless potential that lies within.

As we delve deeper into this transformative journey, we encounter the challenging phase, the Dark Night of the Soul, described by St. John of the Cross. This phase is a crucial, yet often arduous, part of our spiritual journey, marked by feelings of desolation, emptiness, and profound inner turmoil.

The Dark Night of the Soul

"The Dark Night of the Soul" is a concept that originates from a poem by St. John of the Cross, a sixteenth-century Spanish mystic. Although deeply rooted in Catholic mysticism, this term has transcended its original religious context and gained widespread recognition in both spiritual and psychological realms. Fundamentally, it describes a phase in one's spiritual journey characterized by intense feelings of desolation, emptiness, and profound inner turmoil.

Typically, this phase begins unexpectedly, marking a period of spiritual desolation and disconnection. During this time, the spiritual practices that previously offered comfort and solace lose their effectiveness, engulfing one in a sense of profound loneliness akin to wandering in an endless, starless night.

Contrary to what one might expect, this challenging phase is actually indicative of significant spiritual growth. It acts as a cleansing process, purging the soul of attachments, illusions, and ego-driven desires. This intense experience of loss compels individuals to confront and discard their inauthentic parts, thus paving the way for a more genuine connection with either the Divine or their true selves.

In the midst of this dark night, individuals often face doubts, fears, and feelings of abandonment. They grapple with existential questions about the existence of a higher power, their own sense of being forsaken, and the purpose of their suffering. This phase is marked by a profound existential crisis, where one might feel as though they are standing on the edge of an immense abyss.

The key to navigating the Dark Night of the Soul lies not in resistance or avoidance but in embracing and exploring its depths. By accepting and sitting with the pain and uncertainty, individuals can discover insights and understandings that were previously hidden. In the depths of this darkness, faint glimmers of light and truth emerge.

This phase does not last indefinitely. Through time, patience, and often with the help of mentors or spiritual guides, individuals eventually emerge from the darkness into a new dawn. This emergence is characterized by a renewed sense of purpose, a deeper spiritual connection, and an unshakeable inner peace. Those who emerge from the dark night often experience a transformation akin to a phoenix rising from ashes.

Individuals who have traversed the Dark Night of the Soul typically find themselves forever changed. They approach life with a newfound depth of understanding, compassion, and humility. Though fraught with pain, the journey imparts invaluable lessons that enrich one's life in countless ways.

Ultimately, the Dark Night of the Soul is a profound and transformative phase in one's spiritual journey. While it is characterized by pain and desolation, it serves a crucial purpose as a crucible for deep inner transformation. By surrendering to this process and seeking understanding within the darkness, one can emerge with a deeper connection to the Divine, a clearer sense of purpose, and an unshakeable inner peace. It stands as a testament to the human spirit's resilience and the ongoing quest for deeper meaning and connection.

Culmination in Spiritual Awakening

Emerging from the Dark Night of the Soul marks a critical turning point in the journey towards realizing "The Real You." Despite its formidable challenges, this stage is essential for spiritual evolution. It leads to a rebirth, where individuals become more resilient, aligned with their authentic selves, and ready to thrive in the newfound freedom and understanding that comes from embracing "The Real You." This transformation is a profound awakening, illuminating the path to a deeper, more authentic existence.

Understanding and Reclaiming Your Inner Power

In life's journey, many find themselves shackled by the weight of fear. This fear, whether overtly acknowledged or lurking in our subconscious, often dictates our actions, inhibits our potential, and curtails our happiness. To truly live life on our terms, it's crucial to understand these fears and work toward reclaiming the power we've unconsciously surrendered.

The Conscious and Subconscious Mind

Imagine an iceberg. The part visible above the water represents our conscious mind, the immediate thoughts, emotions, and memories we're aware of at any moment. This is the face we present to the world, shaped by societal norms, personal experiences, and immediate desires. It is, in essence, the mask that defines our identity.

Beneath the water, the iceberg expands vastly, symbolizing our subconscious mind. Here lie the long-standing beliefs, past traumas, and deep-seated fears embedded over time, especially during our formative years. The subconscious mind acts like a storage vault, using these pre-recorded tapes to influence our perceptions, reactions, and decisions.

One of the most significant sources of our anxieties is the incessant need to control outcomes. We fear the unknown; to mitigate that, we try to dictate how events should unfold. This desire stems from past experiences and the subconscious scripts telling us that specific outcomes are undesirable or threatening. Thus, we construct barriers, set limitations, and deviate from paths that might lead us toward these feared experiences, missing out on valuable lessons.

Every time we act out of fear, we cede a bit of our inherent power. By not trusting the journey and the innate wisdom of life, we divert our energy into constructing safeguards, often missing the essence of the experience itself. This constant diversion drains us, making us feel less capable and more reliant on external factors for validation.

But here's the transformative realization: fear, in many ways, is a construct. We've bought into a narrative based on societal pressures or past experiences. Recognizing this is the first step toward empowerment. Instead of being enslaved by fear, we can view challenges as lessons, embrace them with gratitude, and trust the larger journey.

Reclaiming your power isn't about becoming invincible or fearless. It's about understanding the sources of your fears, challenging the validity of those fears, and making conscious choices to act from a place of trust and self-belief. In this journey of introspection and growth, remember you are far more potent and resilient than you've been led to believe. Embrace that truth, and watch your life transform.

Chapter 12 | The Tao and the Art of Surrender

"Nature does not hurry, yet everything is accomplished." – Lao Tzu

We often turn to various philosophical and spiritual teachings in our quest to understand life and the universe. Among these, Taoism emerges as a beacon of profound insight, guiding us on the path to harmony and understanding. This chapter delves deep into the essence of Taoist principles, focusing primarily on "The Way" (Tao) and "Wu Wei" and their pivotal roles in mastering life through heightened awareness.

The Tao: The Path of Natural Flow

Taoism, rooted in ancient Chinese wisdom, presents a spiritual tradition that sees the ultimate reality, the Tao, as the foundational source and essence of all existence. More than just a concept, the Tao is a path, not merely to be followed but to be experienced and embraced in its entirety. It invites us to align with the world's natural flow, embodying simplicity, spontaneity, and serenity. This alignment with the Tao is vital to achieving a life of balance and harmony, guiding us to live in accordance with the universe's natural rhythms.

At the heart of Taoist philosophy lies the enigmatic concept of "Wu Wei," which translates to "non-doing" or "effortless action." This principle is not about passivity but about engaging in actions in perfect harmony with the universe's flow. It's an approach to life that emphasizes actions performed without force, without resistance, a way of finding the natural rhythm in every situation and responding with ease and effectiveness. Wu Wei teaches us to act with minimalistic, intuitive effort, emerging from a profound harmony with the Tao.

The Taoist Essence: "The Way" and "Wu Wei"

Taoism, an ancient Chinese philosophy, presents a perspective that emphasizes living in harmony with the Tao, which translates to "The Way ." Tao is not easily defined, as it encompasses everything and nothing simultaneously; it is the natural order of the universe, the essence and fundamental nature of existence. Delving deeper into Taoist philosophy, we encounter two profound concepts: "The Way" (Tao) and "Wu Wei".

The Tao is often described as a path, but it's more than just a road to be traveled; it's the universe's intrinsic nature. The Tao Te Ching, a foundational text of Taoism, starts with the lines: "The Tao that can be told is not the eternal Tao; The name that can be named is not the eternal name." This signifies that Tao is beyond comprehension, description, or definition; it is the mysterious force behind all creation and the fundamental principle that flows through all life.

Imagine a river that flows seamlessly, its water following a course determined by the natural lay of the land. The river doesn't resist its path; it simply follows it. This river is a metaphor for the Tao, a representation of the universe's natural flow and rhythm.

Often translated as "non-action" or "effortless action," Wu Wei is not an endorsement of passivity or inactivity. Rather, it's a call to embrace a form of action that is in harmony with the natural order of things, the Tao. It's about acting with an innate sense of balance without exerting force or encountering resistance. Alan Watts aptly described it as akin to "non-interference," a nuanced understanding of this principle.

To fully comprehend the subtle beauty of Wu Wei, consider the simple yet profound example of a tree. Observe how a tree grows: it does not strain or toil to reach the sky; it effortlessly grows, guided by an intrinsic blueprint. Similarly, birds do not laboriously endeavor to fly; they simply spread their wings and take to the skies. This effortless existence, devoid of struggle, encapsulates the essence of Wu Wei. It's a state where actions are not forced but flow naturally, in perfect sync with the underlying rhythm of the universe. In Wu Wei, there is an elegant simplicity, a graceful unfolding of life's processes, embodying the serenity and power of moving with, not against, the currents of nature.

Integrating "The Way" and "Wu Wei" into Life

Incorporating these Taoist principles into life is a journey toward inner harmony and balance. By understanding and aligning oneself with the Tao, we can approach life's challenges and joys with a serene heart and an accepting mind.

Living by Wu Wei means recognizing when to act or remain still, when to speak or remain silent. It's about letting go of forced efforts and control, allowing life to unfold organically.

By integrating the Tao and Wu Wei into our daily existence, we find a path of least resistance. This doesn't mean avoiding challenges but facing them with a calm spirit and an understanding that the universe has its own flow.

"The Way" and "Wu Wei" provide profound insights into living a life of balance and harmony. They teach us to navigate the complexities of existence with ease, grace, and a deep connection to the universe's rhythms. In embracing these Taoist principles, we find peace within ourselves and cultivate a harmonious relationship with the world.

Peeling the Layers of Consciousness

Our exploration of Taoism would be incomplete without a deep dive into the concept of consciousness. Here, we liken the levels of human consciousness to the layers of an onion. The outermost layer represents basic awareness, a fundamental understanding of oneself and the immediate world. This initial stage of consciousness is where we all start aware but perhaps not fully comprehending the depths of our existence.

As we peel back these layers, moving deeper, we discover more profound levels of consciousness. Each layer peeled away uncovers a richer, more insightful understanding of ourselves and the universe. We begin to perceive life's subtleties, recognizing the interconnectedness of all things. This journey towards the core of the Tao enhances our awareness, leading us towards a more enlightened understanding of our place in the world.

In this section, we embark on a journey through these layers of consciousness. We will explore how each level brings us closer to the

Tao and how the principles of Wu Wei can guide us in this spiritual voyage. Our exploration reveals that mastering life is less about overcoming external challenges and more about aligning with the universe's natural rhythms. This journey is not just a philosophical exploration but a practical guide to living a life of harmony, wisdom, and profound understanding.

Adding Depth to Taoist Wisdom

Understanding Taoist principles, especially "The Way" and "Wu Wei," requires recognizing their roles in mastering life through heightened awareness. These concepts teach us to immerse ourselves fully in life's experiences while maintaining harmony with the universe's natural rhythms, ultimately leading to a state of enlightenment.

Exploring human consciousness is akin to peeling an onion, revealing multiple layers that offer deeper insights as we delve further. This journey begins with basic awareness and gradually progresses toward a more enlightened state of being. We traverse through stages such as naive wonder, conformity, questioning, acceptance, and detachment, each representing a deeper and more evolved state of consciousness. This progression moves us from simple awareness to a mature, enlightened understanding of ourselves and the universe.

As we explore these stages, we uncover the transformative journey of consciousness, moving from an initial, basic awareness of the world to a profound, enlightened understanding of oneself and the universe. This exploration is not just about gaining knowledge; it's about experiencing a transformation that elevates our understanding of life and existence to new heights.

First, there's the "mode of mere existence." This phase is about fundamental awareness or the fundamental state of being conscious. Think of it as being awake and aware of your surroundings without deeper reflection or understanding of your experiences.

Secondly, we have the "enlightened way of being." This phase goes beyond mere awareness. It involves a higher level of consciousness, where one recognizes their existence and understands the deeper aspects of their thoughts, emotions, and the world around them. This is a more reflective and insightful state, where one is not just existing but also actively interpreting and finding meaning in their experiences.

Understanding human consciousness involves exploring these two phases: starting from basic awareness and moving towards a more enlightened, reflective understanding of our existence.

The exploration of human consciousness becomes increasingly intricate as we delve into its developmental stages, much like peeling the complex layers of an onion.

1. **Origins of Wonder (Naive Wonder)**: This is the initial level of consciousness. Like a blank slate or tabula rasa, individuals at this stage are driven by basic curiosity and wonder about the world. Their consciousness is in its most fundamental form, absorbing experiences and sensations without deeper understanding or questioning.
2. **Formation of Beliefs (Conformity)**: As experiences accumulate, individuals form beliefs influenced by societal norms and fears. This level signifies a shift from mere observation to adopting structured thought patterns. However, these beliefs can be limiting, keeping consciousness in a state of conformity and often suppressing deeper potential.
3. **Quest for Enlightenment (Questioning and Seeking)**: Individuals start breaking away from previously accepted beliefs and norms at this level. There's a profound shift towards questioning and seeking deeper truths. This stage represents a more enlightened state of consciousness, focusing on personal growth, understanding, and wisdom beyond societal constructs.
4. **Embrace Total Acceptance (Acceptance and Understanding)**: This stage is marked by a high level of consciousness where individuals learn to accept and embrace experiences, understanding their inherent value fully. It's a state of matured consciousness that recognizes the purpose and lesson in every experience, leading to emotional and spiritual growth.

5. **The Power of Letting Go (Detachment and Wisdom)**: The highest level of consciousness is characterized by the ability to let go and maintain a balanced indifference. It embodies wisdom and understanding of life's dualities. This stage resonates with Stoic principles, focusing on what can be controlled, reactions and interpretations, rather than external events.

Each level represents a deeper and more evolved state of consciousness. The journey through these levels is transformative, moving from an initial, naive awareness of the world to a mature, enlightened understanding of oneself and the universe. It's a progression from simple awareness to deep introspection, acceptance, and, ultimately, wisdom.

By subdividing the topic into these detailed sections, we can offer a more comprehensive and in-depth exploration of the fascinating journey through the levels of human consciousness.

The Liberation of Letting Go: Achieving Harmony with the Tao

In the realm of Taoist philosophy, the concept of "letting go" emerges as a pivotal practice that leads to profound personal transformation and alignment with the universe. This act of releasing, far from being a passive surrender, is a conscious embrace of life's flow, a step towards attaining a deeper connection with the Tao.

Letting go, in Taoism, is not about indifference or neglect; it's about liberating oneself from the bindings of ego, desire, and preconceived notions. It's an active process of releasing attachment to outcomes, personal biases, and the need for control. This liberation opens the door to a state of freedom where one can truly experience the essence of Wu Wei, the art of effortless action.

The process of letting go initiates a profound transformation. By releasing our grip on fixed ideas and rigid expectations, we allow ourselves to flow with the natural rhythms of life. This shift in perspective brings about a deeper understanding and acceptance of the impermanence and interconnectivity of all things. As we let go, we find ourselves more in tune with the universe, experiencing a harmonious blend of action and non-action.

The outcome of this practice is a life lived in harmony with the Tao. When we let go, we align our actions, thoughts, and emotions with the universe's natural order. This alignment results in a life of simplicity, authenticity, and true purpose. Actions arise not from a place of force or desire but from a deep resonance with the Tao.

In this state, we experience a profound inner peace and a sense of unity with all that exists. Challenges and obstacles are met with equanimity and grace, and life's unpredictable turns are navigated with ease and wisdom. Letting go becomes not just a practice but a way of being, deeply rooted in the wisdom of Taoist philosophy.

Embodying the Tao in Daily Life

As we embrace the practice of letting go, we begin to embody the principles of Taoism in our daily lives. Our interactions become more genuine and less forced, our decisions more intuitive and less calculated. We become a living embodiment of Wu Wei, acting with spontaneity and grace, and our existence becomes a testament to the transformative power of Taoist teachings.

In essence, letting go is the key to unlocking a life of true freedom and harmony. It is the gateway to experiencing the universe in its fullest, most vibrant form and a step toward realizing our true potential in alignment with the Tao.

In embodying the Tao in our daily lives through the practice of letting go, we set the stage for a deeper exploration into the realms of personal philosophy and spirituality. This natural progression from Taoist principles brings us to an intriguing juncture: the concept of ambivalence. Just as we have learned to let go and align our actions with the Tao, embodying Wu Wei in our interactions and decisions, we now venture into a territory where expectations are not merely managed but transcended.

Our journey thus far has prepared us for this exploration of ambivalence, where we delve into it not as a conflict of emotions but as a vital philosophical and spiritual practice. This perspective, akin to our understanding of Wu Wei, involves deriving satisfaction not from the fulfillment of specific expectations but from a broader acceptance of life's experiences in their authentic, unmodified state. Drawing from the rich tapestry of wisdom traditions and psychological theories, the next chapter promises to illuminate a path to more profound inner peace and fulfillment, much like our journey through Taoist principles has done.

Ambivalence and Amor Fati: The Western Parallel

The principles of Taoism (Wu Wei, The Way, effortless action) find their precise counterpart in the Western philosophical tradition. What the Taoist calls "going with the flow," the philosopher Friedrich Nietzsche called Amor Fati: the love of fate. Ambivalence, in the deepest philosophical sense, is not passive indifference; it is an active, open-hearted stance toward whatever life presents. Together, Wu Wei and Amor Fati form a single wisdom spoken in two languages.

Ambivalence, in its truest sense, represents a balanced, open-hearted stance toward life's experiences. It transcends the dualities of preference and aversion, desire and rejection. This chapter examines how this concept has been interpreted and valued across cultures and philosophies, from Eastern traditions like Taoism and Buddhism to Western existentialism, revealing its timeless relevance.

We probe the human inclination to control outcomes and how this often leads to dissatisfaction. Letting go of expectations emerges as a path to freedom, differentiating between healthy acceptance and passive resignation. Ambivalence, thus, becomes an active choice of trust and openness, not a surrender to circumstances.

Ambivalence in Everyday Life

The chapter then transitions into practical applications of ambivalence in daily life. It offers methods like mindfulness, reflective journaling, and detached decision-making. We address common challenges in adopting this mindset and strategies to navigate them, offering a guide to incorporating ambivalence into daily routines.

Delving into the psychological realm, we uncover how ambivalence contributes to reduced anxiety and stress, supported by research and theories. It fosters emotional well-being, resilience, and overall happiness, painting a picture of the far-reaching benefits of this mindset.

We explore its significance in spiritual journeys by connecting ambivalence to various spiritual teachings. This section discusses how practicing ambivalence deepens one's connection with the self and the universe, offering a spiritual perspective.

"Amor Fati" in Nietzsche's Philosophy

"Amor Fati," a Latin phrase meaning "love of fate," is a central tenet in the German philosopher Friedrich Nietzsche's philosophy. This concept bridges the Eastern philosophies of ambivalence and Wu Wei and Western existential thought. Nietzsche's "Amor Fati" is not just about acceptance but a deep, passionate love for every aspect of our life's journey.

Nietzsche challenges us not only to accept but to love everything that happens, seeing the beauty and value in every experience, whether it's perceived as good or bad. This radical acceptance and love for life in all its forms aligns closely with the practice of ambivalence and Wu Wei, where we learn to flow with life's rhythms without resistance.

As conceptualized by Nietzsche, "Amor Fati" philosophy invites us to a profound engagement with life beyond mere acceptance. It embodies a perspective where we view all our experiences as integral to our growth and personal evolution. Let's delve deeper into the key points of this philosophy:

1. **Deep Trust in Life's Design:** "Amor Fati" centers on a profound trust in life's process. It's an active faith that every experience, no matter its nature, is part of a larger, meaningful design. This perspective views life as a tapestry woven from a myriad of experiences, each thread vital to the overall picture. Nietzsche's philosophy invites us to trust that every event, whether it brings joy or sorrow, contributes in some way to our growth and evolution.

2. **Active Participation in Life:** Nietzsche suggests that we are not just passive recipients of life's experiences but active participants in shaping them. While we may not have control over every event, our reactions and interpretations are crucial in how these events influence our journey. "Amor Fati" empowers us to see ourselves as co-creators of our life story, actively engaging with whatever life presents us rather than viewing ourselves as victims of external circumstances.
3. **Viewing Experiences as Opportunities:** In this philosophy, every moment of life is seen as an opportunity for personal development. Joyful experiences are not just moments to be enjoyed but also opportunities to cultivate gratitude and presence. On the other hand, difficult experiences are not mere obstacles but invaluable chances for growth. These challenging times are seen as the crucibles that shape our character, build resilience, and deepen our understanding of life.
4. **Learning from Every Encounter:** "Amor Fati" posits that there is a valuable lesson to be learned from every life encounter. Whether it's a challenging relationship, a professional setback, or a personal loss, each experience has the potential for learning and growth. These lessons might relate to discovering our inner strength, learning the art of letting go, understanding the transient nature of life, or recognizing the importance of patience and perseverance.
5. **The Role of Reflection and Mindfulness:** Embracing "Amor Fati" requires a reflective and mindful approach to life. It involves regularly pausing to contemplate the significance of our experiences, understanding their roles in our personal narrative, and recognizing the lessons they impart. This reflective practice allows us to glean wisdom from our experiences, integrating this wisdom into our life's journey.
6. **Embracing Life Wholeheartedly:** Ultimately, "Amor Fati" is a call to embrace life in all its facets with a heart full of trust and faith. It is about finding beauty and purpose in the full spectrum of human experiences and recognizing that each moment, whether filled with joy or pain, contributes

meaningfully to the narrative of our lives. This philosophy encourages us to not only endure life's challenges but to love them, to find meaning in every experience, and to use each as a catalyst for our personal development and learning.

Nietzsche's "Amor Fati" presents a philosophy that resonates deeply with the concepts of ambivalence and Wu Wei, encouraging a joyful acceptance of life's entire cycle. It invites us to embrace life's dance with a loving, open heart, engaging with our experiences passionately and purposefully. This approach to life is not just about passively accepting what comes our way, but rather, it involves actively finding joy and purpose in every moment, viewing each experience as an essential part of our unique journey.

This philosophy urges us to wholeheartedly embrace our life's narrative, recognizing the harmony and beauty in the highs and lows, the calm and the storm. It aligns seamlessly with the principles of ambivalence and Wu Wei, which advocate for a balanced approach to life's unfolding events, one free from resistance and filled with acceptance and understanding.

This perspective of embracing life with an open and loving heart beautifully leads us into a metaphor that vividly captures the essence of our existence: life as a vast, ever-changing voyage. Much like sailing the open seas, life is a journey of exploration and discovery, filled with moments of tranquility and times of turbulence. It's in this journey that we find the true spirit of "Amor Fati": the art of loving our fate, embracing each wave and wind as an integral part of our voyage, and navigating the vast seas of existence with resilience and grace.

Life's Voyage: Sailing the Seas of Existence

The metaphor of life's voyage, akin to sailing the seas of existence, offers a rich, textured narrative that profoundly mirrors the human experience. This analogy allows us to explore the intricacies of our journey through life, likening it to the multifaceted and unpredictable nature of a sailor's journey across the vast ocean.

The ocean, in its immense expanse, represents the vastness and variety of life itself. It's an endless horizon of experiences, encompassing serene tranquility and overwhelming turbulence. Just as the ocean's surface can change from calm to stormy, our lives, too, fluctuate between periods of peace and periods of challenge. Each phase, whether calm or turbulent, serves a purpose in the larger context of our existence.

Akin to how a sailor uses the sails to capture the wind's power, steering the ship towards its destination, we harness our inner strengths, ambitions, and the opportunities that life presents to navigate our path. This process is akin to setting our personal sails: aligning our goals, motivations, and actions to propel us forward. It involves deeply understanding our strengths, weaknesses, desires, and fears and using this knowledge to maneuver through life's complexities.

The unpredictability of the winds on the sea mirrors the uncertainties of life. At times, favorable winds, or fortuitous circumstances, swiftly carry us towards our goals. These are the moments when everything seems to align perfectly, and progress feels seamless. Conversely, we also encounter challenges akin to facing headwinds that test our resilience and determination. These times require us to trust our abilities and the journey, recognizing that these challenges are integral to our growth. Instead of lamenting the adverse winds, the wise sailor learns to adjust the sails, working creatively and resourcefully with the conditions.

The Moods of the Sea and Confronting Life's Storms: Steering Clear of the Past

The ever-changing moods of the sea serve as a poignant metaphor for the fluctuating scenarios of life. Much like unforeseen storms that disturb the ocean's tranquility, life often confronts us with unexpected challenges and obstacles. While some of these difficulties can be anticipated and avoided, there are times when we must confront them head-on. This metaphor illuminates the importance of not resisting or fighting against life's overwhelming forces. Like a steadfast ship braving a tempest, we learn to navigate life's turbulent waters with resilience and adaptability.

An integral part of this journey involves understanding that we cannot live anchored in the past. Just as a boat is not steered by its wake, our lives should not be guided by what lies behind us. The past, with its successes and failures, joys and sorrows, is like the trail left by a ship on the sea; it shows where we have been but does not dictate our future direction. We must learn to sail forward, using past lessons as wisdom to navigate the present, not as anchors that hold us back.

The ultimate wisdom of this voyage lies in flowing with the water and the wind, adapting to the situation without resistance. This approach involves relinquishing the need for control and understanding life's inherent rhythm and flow. As the water effortlessly yields to the forces around it and the winds shift direction, we also must cultivate flexibility and resilience. We achieve a harmonious balance by moving with, rather than against, life's currents. This equilibrium ensures that we remain resolute and focused regardless of our challenges, steering our lives with clarity and purpose, unburdened by the weight of our past.

The Congruence with "Amor Fati"

Drawing parallels between Nietzsche's "Amor Fati" and a sailor's journey, we find a profound alignment. Both perspectives encourage us to embrace life's unpredictability and diversity. They teach us to love our fate, find joy and meaning in both the tranquil and the tumultuous moments, and navigate life with the wisdom and respect of a sailor who understands and works harmoniously with the sea's ever-changing nature.

This metaphorical voyage, underscored by the philosophy of "Amor Fati," becomes a testament to our capacity for growth, adaptation, and finding profound meaning in every twist and turn of our existence. It's a journey that asks us to embrace every aspect of life, to learn from each experience, and to find a balance that keeps us steady and purposeful on our individual paths.

As we delve into the intricate alignment between Friedrich Nietzsche's concept of "Amor Fati" (the love of one's fate) and the journey of a sailor embracing the unpredictability and diversity of life, we find ourselves drawn towards another domain where the unpredictable nature of existence is meticulously examined. This domain is the realm of artificial intelligence (AI) and consciousness. This transition from the metaphorical and philosophical insights of

Nietzsche and the age-old wisdom of seafaring to the tangible and scientific world of AI represents a significant shift in our exploration of life's uncertainties.

Nietzsche's "Amor Fati" encourages a wholehearted acceptance of all life entails: joys, sorrows, triumphs, and failures. It's akin to a sailor who, rather than resisting the capricious winds and tides, learns to embrace them as integral parts of the voyage. In the realm of AI, this concept of embracing unpredictability finds a unique expression in the exploration of machine consciousness and the nature of sentient thought.

Note to the reader: The question of whether consciousness itself is a kind of simulation, whether the observer who collapses quantum possibilities is in turn observed by something greater, opens a philosophical frontier that this trilogy continues to explore. The Dream of Life, the third volume of this series, takes up that question in full.

Chapter 13 | Embracing the Game of Life: The Path to Self-Liberation

"Man is not the creature of circumstances; circumstances are the creatures of men." – Benjamin Disraeli

"Chapter 13: Embracing the Game of Life: The Path to Self-Liberation" delves deep into the heart of the human experience, offering a transformative perspective on our role in shaping our lives. Inspired by Benjamin Disraeli's insightful notion that "Man is not the creature of circumstances, circumstances are the creatures of men," this chapter presents a compelling argument for our active role in creating our reality. It emphasizes that life is not a passive experience where events simply happen to us. Instead, it is a dynamic and interactive game where our experiences, emotions, and choices intertwine to create the tapestry of our existence.

As we navigate through the chapter, we are encouraged to view ourselves as conscious creators, actively participating in the construction of our life's narrative. This realization is empowering and challenging, placing the onus on us to take responsibility for our lives. The chapter explores how our perceptions, attitudes, and decisions not only influence our personal journey but also contribute to the collective human experience. It prompts us to recognize that every thought, emotion, and action we engage in plays a part in sculpting the reality we experience.

The narrative of this chapter takes us through various aspects of self-liberation. It begins by challenging the notion of life as a predestined path determined by external forces. Instead, it introduces the concept of life as an interactive game where each player has the potential to shape their journey. This perspective encourages us to reassess our approach to life's challenges and opportunities, viewing them not as mere obstacles or strokes of luck but as integral parts of a larger, self-directed narrative.

As we delve deeper, the chapter emphasizes the importance of self-awareness in this process. Understanding our desires, fears, motivations, and the underlying patterns of our behavior becomes crucial in this game of life. Through this understanding, we gain the power to make informed choices, break free from limiting beliefs, and steer our lives in directions that resonate with our true selves.

Furthermore, the chapter discusses the balance between accepting what we cannot change and changing what we can. It navigates the fine line between surrender and control, highlighting the wisdom in recognizing the difference. This understanding is vital in the game of life, as it helps us focus our energies on what we can influence, leading to more meaningful and fulfilling experiences.

In summary, "Embracing the Game of Life: The Path to Self-Liberation" is a chapter that calls for a profound shift in how we perceive and interact with our world. It invites us to step into a more active, conscious role where we acknowledge our capacity to shape our reality. This shift is not just about personal empowerment; it's about recognizing that life is a dynamic game of creation, interaction, and transformation in which we are all active participants. The chapter challenges us to embrace this role, engage with life's complexities, and find liberation in realizing that we are the architects of our destiny.

The Role of the Creator

"The Role of the Creator" in this section heralds a pivotal shift in perspective, urging us to embrace the powerful realization that we are the creators of our own reality. This transformative shift challenges the traditional belief that life is merely a sequence of random, uncontrollable events. Instead, it presents life as a complex and intricate tapestry, where every thread (representing our actions, thoughts, and intentions) is woven together to create the broader picture of our existence.

This paradigm shift signifies a profound awakening. It is an acknowledgment that we are not merely passive observers in life's journey but active participants, indeed co-authors, of our own story. This section underscores the idea that every decision we make, every emotion we feel, and every experience we encounter plays a crucial role in shaping our lives. It's a recognition that our daily choices and actions, no matter how small, have significant impacts on the trajectory of our narratives.

In embracing this role as creators, we undergo a transformation in mindset. We begin to see ourselves as architects of our destiny rather than victims of circumstance. This new awareness brings with it a sense of empowerment and responsibility. Understanding that we have a hand in crafting our reality, we become more mindful of our decisions and actions. We start to recognize the power of our thoughts and beliefs in shaping our experiences and, consequently, our reality.

Furthermore, this section delves into the idea that being a creator is not just about shaping our external world but also about crafting our internal landscape. It suggests that how we perceive the world, interpret events, and respond to challenges is also part of our creative process. We can consciously use our internal dialogue, emotions, and attitudes to mold our experiences and influence our journey.

In summary, "The Role of the Creator" is a call to embrace our inherent power to shape our lives. It encourages us to move beyond seeing ourselves as mere products of our environment or victims of fate. Instead, it invites us to step into the role of conscious creators, actively shaping our reality through our choices, beliefs, and attitudes. This section is a powerful reminder of our potential to influence our personal journey and the broader narrative of our lives, empowering us to take ownership and create a life that resonates with our deepest values and aspirations.

Karma and Energy Patterns

"Karma and Energy Patterns" in this section delves into the complex and nuanced concept of karma, a principle deeply embedded in Eastern philosophies. This section explores how karma, often misunderstood, is not a system of punishment or reward but rather a reflection of the accumulation of energy patterns created by our actions, intentions, and choices. These energy patterns, shaped by our past and present behaviors and thoughts, are believed to significantly influence the unfolding narrative of our lives.

Every action we take, every intention we hold, and every choice we make leaves an energetic imprint. This imprint, or karma, then influences future experiences. Karma is seen as a continuum, a cycle where past actions affect present circumstances, which in turn set the stage for future experiences. This cyclical nature of karma underscores the interconnectedness of our actions and their consequences, painting a picture of life where nothing exists in isolation.

In exploring the concept of karma, the section leads us to a crucial realization: the importance of reconciling our past experiences and emotions. It highlights that unresolved emotional attachments and past experiences often act as invisible forces, influencing our current situation and potentially hindering our journey toward self-liberation. These unresolved issues can create patterns that repeat themselves, trapping us in cycles that may seem beyond our control.

The section emphasizes the importance of acknowledging these emotional attachments. It guides us through understanding and releasing them, a process vital for breaking free from negative karmic patterns. Letting go of these attachments is not just about forgetting or suppressing past experiences; it's about confronting them, understanding their impact, and consciously choosing to move beyond them.

This process of reconciliation and release is depicted as a path to achieving a harmonious flow in life. By addressing and resolving our past, we clear the way for positive energy to flow, paving the way for new experiences and opportunities. This harmonious flow is not just about external circumstances but also about achieving inner peace and balance.

In summary, "Karma and Energy Patterns" provides a profound insight into how our actions and intentions shape our life's journey. It presents karma as a complex interplay of energy patterns, emphasizing our choices' significance and long-term impacts. The section encourages a deep introspection into our past experiences and emotions, guiding us toward a path of healing and liberation. It teaches us that by understanding and reconciling our past, we can unlock the potential for a more harmonious and fulfilling future, both internally and externally.

Flowing with Life's Transience: The Art of Letting Go

"Flowing with Life's Transience: The Art of Letting Go" in this section delves into the profound yet often challenging concept of life's inherent impermanence. This section enlightens us on the transient nature of existence, where change is the only constant. In a world where nothing remains static, this section encourages a radical shift in our approach to life, urging us to find satisfaction in the journey rather than in attaining specific, often fleeting outcomes.

The section explores the Buddhist concept of impermanence, which teaches that all things are in a continuous state of flux. This understanding can initially seem unsettling, as human nature often craves stability and predictability. However, the section guides us not only to accept but also to embrace this transition. By doing so, we open ourselves to the richness of life's experiences, learning to appreciate the beauty of each passing moment.

A crucial aspect of embracing impermanence is letting go of our rigid attachments, especially to specific outcomes or expectations. Our society often teaches us to strive for certain goals and to cling to particular ideas of success and happiness. This section, however, suggests a different path, one where we release these stringent expectations and attachments. In doing so, we cultivate a mindset of contentment and peace, finding joy in the flow of life rather than in a relentless pursuit of specific endpoints.

By releasing our grip on expectations and learning to flow with the changing tides of life, we free ourselves from the constant craving for permanence. This detachment does not mean disengagement from life; rather, it's about engaging more fully with life in all its impermanence, savoring the present moment without the weight of needing it to last forever or to unfold in a certain way.

This embrace of impermanence leads to a profound sense of liberation. It allows us to live more fully, to appreciate the beauty of life's ephemerality, and to experience a deeper level of peace and contentment. We learn to appreciate life's fleeting moments of joy, to gracefully accept its sorrows, and to see the beauty in the natural ebb and flow of existence.

In summary, "Flowing with Life's Transience: The Art of Letting Go" is an invitation to a more liberated and peaceful way of living. It challenges us to shift our perspective, let go of our attachments to specific outcomes, and find contentment in life's impermanent nature. This section provides a roadmap for navigating life with a sense of grace and ease, encouraging us to appreciate the journey itself, with all its twists and turns, as the true essence of living.

Stoicism: The Path of Indifference and Acceptance

In this insightful section, we delve into the ancient philosophy of Stoicism, focusing on its core principles of indifference and acceptance. Stoicism, a school of thought originating in ancient Greece, teaches the cultivation of a mental state where emotional responses are tempered by reason and detachment. This philosophy is not about suppressing emotions but about understanding and directing them in a way that aids personal growth and resilience.

At the heart of Stoicism is the practice of indifference, which refers to maintaining a calm and balanced state of mind regardless of external circumstances. This form of indifference is not about apathy or disengagement from the world. Instead, it's about recognizing what is within our control and what is not and responding to the latter with a sense of acceptance. Stoics believe that much of our discontent and frustration arises from trying to control or resist things that are inherently beyond our influence, such as the behavior of others, societal norms, or certain life events.

Acceptance plays a critical role in Stoic philosophy. It involves embracing life's experiences as they are, without excessive judgment or emotional turmoil. Stoicism teaches that while we cannot always control external events, we can control our perceptions and reactions to them. This perspective encourages a deeper understanding of our responses to life's challenges and advocates for a reasoned approach to life's vicissitudes.

Stoicism's approach to indifference and acceptance also involves understanding the impermanence of life and the transience of both joy and sorrow. By maintaining a level of detachment, we are better equipped to handle life's ups and downs. This doesn't mean that Stoics are devoid of feeling but rather that they strive to approach life with a sense of equanimity and composure.

Furthermore, this section explores how the Stoic principles of indifference and acceptance can be applied in modern life. It offers insights into how adopting a Stoic mindset can lead to a more fulfilled and less stressful existence. By learning to differentiate between what we can change and what we must accept, we can lead lives characterized by greater tranquility and effectiveness.

In summary, "Stoicism: The Path of Indifference and Acceptance" presents a compelling exploration of how Stoic principles can guide us to a deeper understanding and mastery of our emotional responses. This section invites us to consider how embracing Stoicism's teachings can transform our approach to life's challenges, leading to a more balanced, composed, and fulfilling existence.

Cultivating Ambivalence: The Art of Non-Control

"Cultivating Ambivalence: The Art of Non-Control" in this section delves into the empowering practice of developing a balanced detachment towards life's myriad outcomes. This concept challenges the often ingrained human desire to exert control over every facet of our existence, proposing an alternative approach that embraces life's inherent unpredictability.

Cultivating ambivalence is about finding a middle ground between attachment and indifference. It's about recognizing that while we can guide and influence our lives to some extent, a great deal remains beyond our direct control. This realization can initially be discomforting, as it confronts the deeply rooted human need for certainty and predictability. However, the section guides us through this transformative journey, showing how releasing our grip on control can lead to a profound sense of peace and acceptance.

We learn to approach life's outcomes with a balanced perspective by fostering ambivalence. Instead of being heavily invested in specific results or being completely indifferent, we find a harmonious state where we are engaged in our pursuits but not overly attached to the results. This state of being allows us to put in our best efforts while being at peace with whatever outcome life presents us. It's about acknowledging life's fluidity and embracing the ebb and flow of experiences.

The release of the need for control opens us up to the beauty and serendipity of life. We start to appreciate the wisdom in allowing events to unfold naturally, without the constant interference of our ego-driven desires. This approach doesn't imply passivity; rather, it's an active choice to live in harmony with the natural course of events, making peace with the fact that not everything can be planned or predicted.

Cultivating ambivalence, as presented in this section, is not just a coping mechanism; it's a profound shift in perspective that can lead to inner tranquility and freedom. It is a gateway to experiencing life in a more relaxed, open, and fulfilling way. By embracing this art of non-control, we learn to navigate life with a sense of calm and confidence, trusting in the journey and finding joy and contentment in the present moment, regardless of external circumstances.

In essence, "Cultivating Ambivalence: The Art of Non-Control" offers a path to a more peaceful and liberated way of living. It encourages us to let go of our illusion of control over life's outcomes and to embrace a more flexible, open-minded approach. This section guides finding balance and tranquility in a world that is often unpredictable and beyond our control.

The Futility of Seeking Outside Ourselves

"The Futility of Seeking Outside Ourselves" in this section addresses a fundamental dilemma in the human experience: the endless pursuit of external validation and fulfillment. This pursuit, deeply ingrained in societal conditioning, drives many to continuously seek approval, success, or material possessions, often at the cost of inner peace and contentment. The section explores this relentless chase and its implications, portraying it as a cycle that frequently leads to dissatisfaction, anxiety, and a sense of never being quite enough.

The narrative of this section is a poignant reflection on the societal pressures that push us to constantly strive to become something else, to achieve more, and to own more, suggesting that happiness and fulfillment are always just beyond our grasp. This constant striving creates a sense of restlessness, where contentment is perpetually deferred to some future achievement or acquisition. The section challenges this notion, arguing that such a pursuit is not only exhausting but fundamentally futile.

In a shift from external seeking to internal exploration, the discussion encourages readers to recognize that what they often seek outside themselves may already reside within. It advocates for an inward transformative journey, suggesting that true fulfillment and a sense of worthiness come from accepting and embracing our inherent qualities and potential. This internal exploration involves recognizing and appreciating our unique essence, strengths, and imperfections.

The section calls for a cessation of the endless quest to transform ourselves according to external standards and to instead recognize our innate worthiness. It posits that the desire to continuously become something else is unattainable and unnecessary. By understanding and accepting ourselves as we are, we can find a deeper sense of satisfaction and peace.

This section is not just an examination of societal influences; it is a call to action. It urges readers to break free from the cycle of external validation and embark on a journey of self-discovery and self-acceptance. It's an invitation to step off the treadmill of constant striving and find fulfillment in being rather than becoming.

In summary, "The Futility of Seeking Outside Ourselves" offers a profound insight into a common human experience, the pursuit of external validation. It challenges readers to redirect their focus inward, to discover and embrace their true selves. This section serves as a guide to finding a deeper sense of fulfillment and peace within, emphasizing the importance of self-acceptance and the recognition of our inherent worthiness.

Embracing Responsibility

"Embracing Responsibility" in this section delves into a transformative concept central to personal empowerment and self-growth: the recognition and acceptance of personal responsibility in creating our life experiences. This idea is intricately linked to embracing the role of the creator in our lives, an acknowledgment that we are not merely passive recipients of external circumstances but active participants in shaping our journey.

At the core of this concept is a profound shift in how we perceive our experiences. By embracing responsibility, we start to see every event in our lives, whether joyous or challenging, as an opportunity for growth and self-realization. This perspective enables us to understand that even experiences perceived as negative hold valuable lessons and are integral to our personal evolution. We begin to trust the process we have initiated, recognizing that each step and decision is part of a larger journey toward self-discovery and fulfillment.

Accepting responsibility for everything in our lives marks a departure from viewing ourselves as victims of circumstance. This change in outlook allows us to see that we possess the power to respond to life's challenges with wisdom, resilience, and grace. It's a realization that our reactions and decisions in the face of adversity are within our control, and these responses can either propel us forward or keep us anchored in unproductive patterns.

This shift in perspective is empowering. It moves us from passivity to active engagement with our lives. We no longer find ourselves at the mercy of external forces; instead, we recognize that we have agency in navigating our path. This empowerment comes with the understanding that our choices, attitudes, and actions play a crucial role in shaping our experiences and, ultimately, our lives.

By embracing this responsibility, we open ourselves to making more conscious choices and decisions that are in harmony with our true selves and deepest values. It allows us to steer our lives in directions that are not only more fulfilling but also more authentic. It is a journey that requires courage and introspection, as it involves confronting aspects of ourselves and our lives that we may have previously shied away from.

In summary, "Embracing Responsibility" is a call to recognize and accept our role as the architects of our experiences. It encourages a profound internal shift from seeing ourselves as passive players to understanding our capacity as active creators of our reality. This section guides us toward a deeper sense of empowerment and self-awareness, highlighting the importance of taking responsibility for our lives and using our innate power to craft a journey that reflects our true aspirations and potential.

"The Nature and Role of Distractions" in this section provides a nuanced understanding of how distractions function in our lives, both as defense mechanisms and as potential catalysts for growth. This exploration into the psychology of distractions examines how the mind often resorts to creating diversions to maintain the status quo and avoid the discomfort of deep introspection and change.

The Essence of Living: Mastery of Life

"The Essence of Living: Mastery of Life" in this section presents a profound and introspective view of existence, where life is portrayed not as a final destination or a series of checkpoints but as an ongoing journey rich with experiences and learning. This perspective shifts the focus from merely achieving specific goals to embracing and mastering the art of living.

In this grand tapestry of existence, each thread represents our experiences, choices, and interactions, which intertwine to shape our understanding of the world and our place within it. This section posits that life should not be seen as a static entity with predetermined paths and outcomes. Instead, it is depicted as a dynamic, ever-evolving narrative continuously written and rewritten through our engagements and decisions.

The section emphasizes the significance of viewing life as a journey, a concept that allows for a more profound appreciation of each moment and experience. It suggests that the true essence of living lies in the process itself: the growth, the challenges, the triumphs, and even the setbacks. Each aspect contributes to the richness and depth of our individual stories.

This perspective encourages a mindset of exploration and curiosity. By seeing life as a journey, we become more open to new experiences, more resilient in the face of challenges, and more adaptable to change. We begin to understand that mastery of life does not lie in rigidly controlling our path but skillfully navigating the winding roads, learning from each twist and turn.

Moreover, the section delves into how our choices and interactions are critical in shaping our life's narrative. Every decision, big or small, every relationship we foster, and every reaction to the events around us adds depth and color to the story of our lives. These elements are not just passive occurrences but active contributions to the ongoing creation of our personal and collective existence.

In essence, "The Essence of Living: Mastery of Life" invites readers to embrace life's journey with all its intricacies. It challenges the conventional pursuit of static goals and destinations, encouraging instead a deeper engagement with the process of living. This section is a call to embrace each moment, find joy and learning in life's experiences, and recognize that mastery of life lies in the art of navigating this beautiful, ever-changing journey.

The Game of Life: Roles and Reactions

"The Game of Life: Roles and Reactions" in this section presents an intriguing metaphor, portraying life as a complex game where each individual learns to navigate and play by its unique set of rules or limitations. This section explores the idea that our life experiences are significantly shaped by how we perceive and interpret the world around us. It draws on the principles of quantum physics to delve into the role of observation in crafting our reality, highlighting the deep interconnection between our consciousness and our experiences.

In this metaphorical game of life, each person assumes various roles, influenced by societal norms, personal beliefs, and individual circumstances. These roles often dictate how we react to different situations, interact with others, and view ourselves within the larger context of the world. The section discusses the importance of understanding these roles and the reactions they elicit, emphasizing that our awareness of them can profoundly impact how we play the game.

The concept of perception and interpretation as the creators of our reality is central to this discussion. Drawing on quantum physics, particularly the idea that the act of observing can affect the observed, it illustrates how our perceptions and thoughts are not merely passive reflections of an objective reality. Instead, they actively participate in shaping that reality. Our consciousness, with its beliefs, expectations, and interpretations, plays a critical role in constructing the experiences we have and the world we inhabit.

This section also delves into the idea that life, much like a game, involves learning, adapting, and, sometimes, redefining the rules. It suggests that as we grow and evolve, our understanding of life's 'game' deepens, and we become more skilled at navigating its complexities. This process of learning and adaptation is not always straightforward; it often involves facing challenges, making mistakes, and adjusting our strategies.

Moreover, the section encourages a shift in perspective from viewing life as a series of random events to seeing it as an interactive and responsive experience. It invites readers to engage more consciously with their roles and reactions, understanding that these elements are crucial in the game of life. By becoming more aware and intentional about our perceptions and responses, we can influence the course of our lives in more meaningful and positive ways.

In summary, "The Game of Life: Roles and Reactions" offers a compelling perspective on life as an interactive and dynamic experience. It encourages readers to understand and embrace their roles, be mindful of their reactions, and recognize their consciousness's power in shaping their reality. This section guides us to see life not as a predetermined path but as a responsive and evolving game in which we have the agency to play an active and meaningful role.

Embracing Our True Selves

"Embracing Our True Selves" in this section provides a refreshing counterpoint to the prevalent culture of relentless self-improvement and perpetual change that dominates much of modern society. In a world that often equates worth with achievement and success, this section advocates a different approach, one that is rooted in the Taoist principle of Wu Wei, or 'effortless action,' which emphasizes the value of letting go and finding harmony in one's inherent nature.

The section begins by examining the pervasive culture of constant striving that characterizes much of contemporary life. In this context, individuals are frequently encouraged to pursue a never-ending cycle of self-improvement, with societal norms and media often dictating standards of success, happiness, and worthiness. This relentless pursuit can lead to a disconnection from one's true self, as the effort to conform to external ideals often overshadows the innate qualities and values of the individual.

Contrasting this with Taoist philosophy, it introduces the concept of embracing our true selves by letting go of forced efforts to change according to external standards. Taoism teaches the art of living in harmony with one's true nature, suggesting that peace and contentment come from aligning with the natural flow of life rather than resisting or trying to control it. This principle encourages a state of being where actions are effortless and arise naturally from one's inherent characteristics.

The discussion encourages readers to shift their focus inward, to explore and accept their authentic selves. It suggests that true fulfillment and contentment come from this acceptance and the subsequent alignment of one's life with one's genuine inner self. This approach does not mean abandoning growth or improvement but redefines these concepts to mean growth that is in harmony with one's true nature rather than growth dictated by external pressures and ideals.

Furthermore, the section delves into the practical aspects of embracing our true selves. It discusses how self-acceptance leads to a more authentic way of living, where decisions and actions are more congruent with one's values and desires. This alignment leads to a more peaceful and satisfying life, as it reduces the internal conflict and stress that often accompany efforts to conform to external expectations.

In summary, "Embracing Our True Selves" is a call to break away from the constant striving culture and rediscover and embrace our inherent nature. It promotes a view of life where contentment and peace are found not in ceaseless self-improvement and change but in accepting and appreciating our authentic selves. This section offers a path to a more harmonious and fulfilling existence, guided by the understanding and acceptance of our true nature and the Taoist principle of effortless action.

Mastery Through Simplicity

"Mastery Through Simplicity," the concluding section of the section, resonates with the profound wisdom imparted by philosopher Alan Watts, emphasizing that the true essence of life is in the mere act of being alive. This final section beautifully encapsulates the journey of the book, guiding readers toward embracing the simplicity inherent in existence and recognizing that true mastery of life comes from engaging with it authentically and wholeheartedly.

The section builds upon the idea that mastery in life doesn't necessarily stem from accumulating knowledge, wealth, or achievements but rather from simplifying our approach to life. It encourages readers to shed the unnecessary baggage of emotional attachments and the complexities that often cloud our existence. By embracing the transient nature of life and letting go of the incessant need to control every aspect of our experiences, we open ourselves to a more serene and fulfilling way of living.

This theme of simplicity is interwoven with the insights gained throughout the book: the acknowledgment of impermanence, the understanding of our role as creators of our reality, and the importance of navigating distractions with mindfulness. It illustrates how these elements can lead to a profound sense of peace and contentment when approached with a sense of simplicity and authenticity.

In this state of simplicity, we learn to savor the richness of each moment, appreciating life's experiences as they are, free from the distortions of ego-driven desires. This approach is not about leading a life devoid of ambition or desire but about finding a balance where our ambitions and desires do not overshadow the simple joys of living.

This should serve as a guiding light on the path to self-awareness and self-liberation. It invites us to step back from the relentless pursuit of external validation and to find joy in the simplicity of being. It teaches us that in the process of embracing our true selves, releasing the need for control, and appreciating life's impermanence, we can discover a more genuine and gratifying way of being.

In conclusion, "Mastery Through Simplicity" offers a powerful message: that the essence of life is found not in the accumulation of experiences or possessions but in the joy of being alive. It is an invitation to embrace the present, to live with an open heart and mind, and to find beauty and fulfillment in the simplicity of existence. This section reminds us that in the simplicity of living authentically and mindfully, we find the deepest form of mastery and the true essence of life.

Epilogue

Chapter 14 | The Man and the Mountain

"Knowing yourself is the beginning of all wisdom." – Aristotle

In a realm where tales were more than mere entertainment, where they were the vessels of profound wisdom, there existed a young student whose soul was alight with an unquenchable thirst for knowledge. This narrative, set in a quaint village where life's rhythms were as serene as the meandering river nearby, unfolds the journey of this boy, whose aspirations soared far beyond the ordinary.

Day after day, with the unwavering regularity of the sun's journey across the sky, the student would sit, engulfed in the aura of his teacher's vast wisdom. One day, this teacher, a beacon of knowledge, narrated a tale that would irrevocably steer the student's life onto a new course.

He told of an aged sage living in solitude on a mountain enveloped in nature's embrace, a place where legends whispered in the wind. Having journeyed through the tapestry of life, this sage had unearthed a profound harmony in the myriad experiences that life offered, from soaring achievements to humbling setbacks.

Enthralled by this narrative, the student felt an inner awakening, a call that resonated with the core of his being. It was a call to embark on a journey that would lead him not just to the sage but to the depths of life's meaning. Driven by a deep yearning to grasp the essence of existence, he left the familiar behind and venturing into the vast unknown.

His journey was a mosaic of experiences, each a vibrant piece shaping his understanding. He traversed distant lands, each with its own rhythm and story, immersing himself in the diversity of life's canvas. He encountered joy and sorrow, love and despair, and witnessed the miracle of birth and the inevitability of death. Through these experiences, he delved into the depths of human emotions, each a lesson, each a reflection of life's multifaceted nature.

As he embarked on this path of discovery, he carried with him the wisdom imparted by his teacher and an unyielding resolve. Unbeknownst to him, this journey was one of profound transformation, leading him to insights far surpassing his initial quest.

Years later, atop the mountain that once seemed an enigmatic destination, the student, matured and sculpted by time and trials, sat in reflective solitude. Here, amidst the grandeur of nature, he was about to realize the culmination of his quest.

Closing his eyes, he let his odyssey's memories flood him. Each face he met, each culture he experienced, and each challenge he overcame had guided him to this pinnacle of truth.

As the day gave way to a golden sunset, a revelation unfurled within him. The wise old man, the beacon of his quest, was not a solitary sage awaiting discovery but a symbol of the wisdom within him. The journey had been inward, a path to discovering the sage within himself.

In this moment of enlightenment, the profound truth unveiled itself: "The creator created you to discover, you are the creator." His life, his journey, was a tapestry of his own creation. Every choice, every challenge, every path was a stroke of his own making. He was not merely a creation of fate; he was a creator, shaping his destiny.

Embracing this wisdom, a serene peace enveloped him. He understood that each experience, whether imbued with joy or tinged with pain, was a vital thread in the fabric of his being. He was both the artist and the canvas, crafting his existence with every thought, every belief, every action.

The man gazed at the stars as night draped the mountain, feeling an intrinsic connection with the cosmos. The sage he sought was not an external entity but a profound truth within his soul. The search for understanding, for purpose, had ultimately led him to himself.

With the cosmos as his witness, he vowed to continue his journey, not in search of external wisdom but as an exploration of his own depths. His path of discovery and creation was an eternal dance with life itself.

The narrative closes with the man descending the mountain, transformed in age and wisdom. He was no longer the student seeking external wisdom but a sage in his own right, a bearer of the mountain's profound lessons. The wisdom he sought had always been within him, awaiting revelation through his life's journey. The student had evolved into the teacher, the creation into the creator, and the journey, boundless and profound, continued ever onward.

Thank you.

REFERENCES

1. "Formal Results: Testing the GCP Hypothesis." Global Consciousness Project. 1998-2015.

2. "Native Spirituality according to Luther Standing Bear." 2008.

3. "Organized religion." Wikipedia.

4. "Religion." Merriam-Webster.

5. "Religion." Dictionary.com.

6. "Science." Dictionary.com.

7. "Science." Cambridge Dictionary.

8. "Socrates." New World Encyclopedia.

9. "The Second Noble Truth: The Noble Truth of the Origin of Dukkha." Access to Insight. 2013.

10. "What does the Bible say about how to find purpose in life?" GotQuestions.org.

11. "What is the Global Consciousness Project?" Global Consciousness Project. 1998-2015.

12. Amundson, Ron. "The Hundredth Monkey Phenomenon." 1985.

13. Bhagavad-Gita Trust. "Chapter 17 Verse 3."

14. Bhikkhu Thanissaro. "Kalama Sutta: To the Kalamas."

15. Bodh Bhikkhu. "The Noble Eightfold Path: The Way to the End of Suffering." Access to Insight. 2013.

16. Campbell, Thomas. My Big TOE: The Complete Trilogy. Lightning Strike Books, 2007.

17. Campbell, Thomas. My Big Toe.

18. Dumoulin, Heinrich. Zen Buddhism: A History India & China. World Wisdom, 2005.

19. Fisher, David James. Romain Rolland and the Politics of Intellectual Engagement. University of California Press, 1988.

20. Meshberger, Frank Lynn. "An Interpretation of Michelangelo's Creation of Adam Based on Neuroanatomy." JAMA: The Journal of the American Medical Association, 1990.

21. Baker, Robert J., and Ronald K. Chesser. "The Chernobyl Nuclear Disaster and Subsequent Creation of a Wildlife Preserve."

Environmental Toxicology and Chemistry, 2000.

22. Lamb, Robert. "What is the anthropic principle?" HowStuffWorks, 2010.

23. Lavine, T.Z. From Socrates to Sartre: The Philosophic Quest. Bantam, 1985.

24. Lipton, Bruce H. The Biology of Belief: Unleashing the Power of Consciousness, Matter & Miracles. Hay House, 2008.

25. Rankin, M.D., Lisa. "The Nocebo Effect: Negative Thoughts Can Harm Your Health." Psychology Today, 2013.

26. Miller, Barbara Stoler. The Bhagavad Gita: Krishna's Counsel In Time of War. QPBC, 1998.

27. Freedman, Rabbi Dr. H., and Maurice Simon. "Midrash Rabbah: Translated Into English."

28. Rovelli, Carlo. "Relational quantum mechanics." International Journal of Theoretical Physics, 1996.

29. Schucman, Helen. A Course In Miracles. Course in Miracles Society, 1972.

30. Ueshiba, Morihei. The Art of Peace. Shambhala, 2002.

31. "Backgrounder on Chernobyl Nuclear Power Plant Accident." USNRC, 2014.

32. Waddington, C. H. The Strategy of the Genes: A Discussion of Some Aspects of Theoretical Biology. George Allen & Unwin, 1957.

33. "What is the Photograph of Frozen Water Crystals?" Masaru Emoto, 2010.

34. Jones, Judy, and William Wilson. An Incomplete Education. Ballantine Books, 2008.

35. "Word Study: Ezer Kenegdo." God's Word to Women

About the Author

Born and raised in a devout Catholic environment, I diligently participated in church services throughout my formative years. While I respected the faith and traditions, I found myself drawn to explore other religious philosophies. Over the years, my intellectual journey led me to delve into Buddhism, Hinduism, Gnosticism, and an even deeper exploration of Christianity. Yet, a sense of fulfillment eluded me in every doctrine and teaching.

As I entered my late forties, a profound introspection began to shape my worldview. I recognized that many of my beliefs were not discovered through my exploration but were imparted to me by external influences. The pivotal moment in my spiritual evolution arose when I reexamined my conception of God. My longstanding belief of a distant creator overseeing and orchestrating the universe no longer resonated with my evolving understanding.

Upon deeper contemplation, I embraced a transformative realization: the divine essence I had been seeking externally was, in fact, innate within me. I no longer viewed life as a series of externally imposed events but rather as a canvas upon which I held the brush. This revelation positioned me as the creator of my reality, fostering a profound sense of peace and empowerment.

It is this transformative journey, this quest for inner peace and purpose, that I wish to share through my writing. I hope that, by sharing my journey, readers may find a path to their inner harmony, embrace their true potential, and discover the enduring peace that lies within.

www.ingramcontent.com/pod-product-compliance
Lightning Source LLC
LaVergne TN
LVHW010702110826
845149LV00014B/3199